Shaking the Olive Tree

Preparation for Revival

By Dalen Garris

This is a work of history. Historical individuals and places and events are mentioned.

Published by Revivalfire Ministries

Cover Artwork by Renee Garris

ISBN 13: 978-1-7377944-1-7

All scripture references are taken from the King James Version

For information:
dale@revivalfire.org

First paperback printing October 2021

Printed in the United States of America

Epigraph

When thus it shall be in the midst of the land among the people, there shall be as the shaking of an olive tree, and as the gleaning grapes when the vintage is done.

(Isaiah 24:13)

And this word, Yet once more, signifieth the removing of those things that are shaken, as of things that are made, that those things which cannot be shaken may remain.

Whose voice then shook the earth: but now he hath promised, saying, Yet once more I shake not the earth only, but also heaven.

(Hebrews 12:26-27)

Table of Contents

Introduction

These newspaper articles were published over the course of a year or so and also sent out to our mailing list. I wrote them as the Lord gave them to me. It was if there was a driving force behind each one to be spoken into the wind and be born.

Now there is another driving force to publish them so that they will be established in these books for an even greater audience. I have no idea what the Lord has planned – when have I ever? – but I am assured that He always has a plan.

My prayer and goal is to see these books spread across the land so that His Word will act as the catalyst to bring revival. The Church is so far from where it should be and once was that without some kind of a calamitous shaking, we will not wake to the repentance we need to prepare us for a revival.

Meet for the Master's Use

The call to bring revival to a nation is not something that can be accomplished through any strength or wisdom that we possess in ourselves. No matter how badly you want to plunge into the fray and proclaim liberty in the land, the power to bring the presence and power of God that will ignite the Church is not something that can be flippantly learned in Seminary or produced with any carnally designed program. Only God can do that. And only in complete surrender are we able to lend ourselves as crucified vessels that He can work through. Frank Bartleman, in recounting an encounter he had with the Lord, wrote that the Lord told him after he had received the Baptism of the Holy Ghost, *"If you were only small enough, I could do anything with you."*

Ah, there lies the crux, almost a Catch-22 if you would. How does one maintain, or better put, achieve that place of true humility so that God can use you to do His mighty works? On the one hand, we strive to get to that place of righteousness to have power in God while at the same time, try to stay in that broken place of humility in God so we can surrender to His power. How does one strike that perfect balance? Sounds simple … but is it?

David had it; Saul did not. Perhaps that was because, for Saul, it was always about Saul. When he was little in his own eyes, he was hiding amongst the stuff, but a couple of years later, he was such a big shot that he didn't think he had to wait on God's prophet to offer the sacrifice. But for David, on the other hand, it was never about David; it was always about God. Because of that, he was able to take on Goliath as a kid, and later on with just a couple of other guys, the entire Philistine army. (2 Samuel 23:9)

Any man of God who has had the power of God work through him will immediately be attacked by the enemy. Whether it is miracle healings, dynamic preaching, or supernatural revelation, no sooner does one experience the touch of God's hand than that little wisp will pass through the back of his mind that, "yes it was God's power, but … ahem … He chose to use you!" Satan will lightly sneak those thoughts in as subtly as he can.

It doesn't take much to recognize the devil's handiwork, so he keeps as light a touch as he can … and then another … and then another, merging them ever so slightly into the several streams of your thoughts until he can find an anchor somewhere in your heart to attach his lines of vanity and plant his seeds of pride.

The challenge that faces a man of God who desires to be used supernaturally lies in how to be "meet for the Master's use" (2 Timothy 2:21) and yet keep his ego and self completely invisible. God does not bestow His power on just anybody. He may work through anybody, but He is careful to whom He entrusts His power. We must be careful that our desire to be used by God is not rooted in our own self-image or desire for position in God, but entirely upon the promotion of the kingdom of God. As 1st Corinthians 13 tells us, you can have the faith to move mountains, but if you do not have charity, it is worth nothing.

Easily said; not so easily achieved. Any fool can spout off religious platitudes that boast of unearned righteousness and spirituality, but it is an entirely different matter to fight your way through the spiritual swamp of fleshly ego and pride to arrive at that place where God can use you.

I often hear young Christians naively spout off that they have been called to be a prophet. My first response is to tell them to pray and beg God to change His mind and please choose someone else because you will die a thousand deaths before you enter into that calling.

Ego, pride, and self-awareness must be burned out of you before you are ready to enter into any place of real power. God will give it to you in pieces – just enough to lift you up so He can break you down again. Line upon line, one step at a time, until you gradually become empty of self. Jacob had his Laban, Joseph his prison, and Moses his desert, and you will have your place of cauterizing fire to take the "you" out of you so God can fill you up with Himself. His goal is not to change you, but to kill you. He wants to purify you into transparent glass so that when people look at you, it is not you that they see, but the fire of God that is in you.

And so, with the power that works through you, there is a deep innate understanding that it is not you but God who is working through you to do miracles. You are nothing but dust and ashes; you don't even own the breath in your body. You are dead in Christ, crucified to the world, numb to pride and arrogance. Any place that Satan could have gotten hold of has been broken away. You have finally surrendered to God.

When you are no longer mindful about yourself or your spiritual place in God, and you just simply do not care anymore, you are finally "meet for the Master's use". Only then are you ready to wield the power of God so that He, and He alone, will get the glory. And only then can He use you to bring revival.

"But in a great house there are not only vessels of gold and of silver, but also of wood and of earth; and some to honor, and some to dishonor. If a

man therefore purge himself from these, he shall be a vessel unto honor, sanctified, and meet for the master's use, and prepared unto every good work."

(2 Timothy 2:20-21)

God Ain't Fair

What happens when bad things happen to good people? Is God not fair who watches over us?

We all want to believe in a fairy-tale existence where life is at least fair if not blessed. We hold on to our Christianity and find an equilibrium in our lives where we are comfortable with our faith in God and expect that all things will work to good for those who love Him and keep His commandments. That's what it says in the Bible, doesn't it? Even though the Bible also says that the heart of man is deceitful and desperately wicked, still, we don't <u>feel</u> overly wicked. We believe in God and go through all the modes of the Christian life that we are expected to be part of, so naturally, we expect good things from God.

But what happens when things don't go the way we expected or at least hoped? Sometimes Life deals us a losing hand that places us in a terrifying situation that doesn't make sense to us. Sometimes, all of a sudden, things aren't so good, and we find ourselves wondering what happened. We know that tragedies happen all the time, but we expect them to happen to someone else, not us. What happens when all of a sudden, the table is turned, and we have nowhere to go for help?

It is easy to talk about holding on to our faith when it's not our faith that is being tested. We can mouth all the platitudes to others who are experiencing a catastrophe, but when it's us who is facing a catastrophe, it can feel like we are grasping thin air in our desperate cries to God for help. This wasn't supposed to happen. Not to us. But it did, and now we are crying out to God for help … but sometimes there is only stillness in the night as we wait for an answer.

Is Life so fickle that there is no telling how the tragedies and triumphs will be dealt to us? Is Life just a roll of the dice? And when it goes bad, where is the answer from God? Job found himself in this situation thousands of years ago and he didn't have any answers either. Joseph faced life in a dungeon, and he hadn't done anything wrong. It must have seemed like he had been abandoned by God.

I have seen hundreds of people healed with just a simple laying on of hands and a prayer. Easy. Nothing to it. God just shows up and heals them on the spot. But I also have friends who lead lives of righteousness and sincerely seek God but who have had debilitating sicknesses for years, and it seems no amount of crying out to God does any good. We all would like a rational explanation for this seeming imbalance, so we come up with fine-sounding sayings to explain it away. But fine-sounding explanations sound hollow to someone who is in desperate need of an answer. Sometimes we hear no answer at all … only silence.

David, in Psalm 37, cries out that he has seen the wicked spreading themselves like a green bay tree but that in the end, they shall meet their judgment, but the righteous will be delivered. This is the ultimate resolution that we all need to believe in, but when we are immersed in a present reality of pain, we need an answer now, not later on the Day of Judgment. We need to know that God hears us and will answer us … and we need to know why we are going through this. Those answers are not always forthcoming, nor are they easy.

Much of it has to do with our spiritual condition. I don't believe that any of us truly understand what our spiritual condition is. Just as water seeks its own level and will rest at a certain spot, so we often find a spiritual level in our lives that we are comfortable with and tend to rest there. We tend to think we're okay. That, however, is not always the place God is satisfied with and He may jar us out of there to squeeze us into a deeper crucified walk than we would ever take ourselves. Being pulled into the sufferings of the Body of Christ is the only way the cloud of flesh can be dissolved so that we can experience the spiritual clarity of a deeper walk in the Spirit. That is something only God can do. We do not possess the power to pierce that veil with our carnal will.

Some people are called into higher callings than others. I have no idea how God makes those determinations, but I know that some people are anointed vessels of God and have been called to bear the power and authority of the Holy Spirit at a deeper level than others. Those are vessels that must go through a deeper refining fire than others. Proverbs 17:3 says, *"The fining pot is for silver, and the furnace for gold: but the LORD trieth the hearts."* Some people are silver, and others are gold. Those who are gold have to go through a stronger furnace to purify them so that they are sanctified and meet for the Master's use.

Sometimes it's as simple as God putting us through extreme trouble just to get our attention or to get us back in line. Ask Jonah what that was like.

I don't know what you are going through right now or what you or I will face later on, but I do firmly believe that God is in complete control. But that is not the problem. We all assume that God knows what is going on -- He might even be the One doing it. What we need to know is if God is hearing us when we cry out to Him and what do we have to do to get Him to answer. That's our real question.

And that has more to do with what our walk in God has been more than anything else.

When your walk in God is deeply rooted in the Spirit, you will still go through the fire, but you will have a hold on the reality of His presence while He walks through it with you. If you are not deeply seated in that secret place in God, then your hold is tenuous at best and your grip on His hand is slippery.

Have you been seeking the face of God with all your heart? Has He been the passion of your life or a hobby that you get to when you have time?

Have you extended your soul out to those in need, especially the lost? Have you answered the call in Isaiah 58 to deal the Bread of Life to the hungry, to break the yokes and lift the heavy burdens of sin, clothe the naked with the robes of righteousness, and take the spiritually homeless into your house of God? If you need mercy in your life, understand that only mercy begets mercy.

Where mercy isn't sowed, mercy isn't growed.

Has your life been like a mirror that has reflected the glory of God or more like a translucent glass that absorbs part of the glow for yourself? How much carnal flesh are you carrying around? Is your vessel as clear as transparent glass so that when people look at you, they don't see you, but they see the fire of God that is in you? Or do you need 21 years of broken subjection like Jacob did to take the Jacob out of Jacob before he could become Israel?

Maybe it is true that God is not fair … but that, my friend, is the mercy of God.

A Brand New Altar

> *Now therefore, behold, the Lord bringeth up upon them the waters of the river, strong and many, even the king of Assyria, and all his glory: and he shall come up over all his channels, and go over all his banks:*
>
> *And he shall pass through Judah; he shall overflow and go over, he shall reach even to the neck; and the stretching out of his wings shall fill the breadth of thy land, O Immanuel."*
>
> *(Isaiah 8:7-8)*

Hezekiah was one of Judah's best kings. 2nd Kings says that there was none like him amongst all the kings of Judah. Then why did this happen to him? Sennacherib, the king of Assyria swallowed up the entire breadth of Judah, reaching all the way up to the neck, even the very gates of Jerusalem. That was good news for the folks shuttered up in Jerusalem, but it must have been hell for everyone out in the countryside and all the other cities. If Hezekiah was so righteous, then why did God allow this to happen to the rest of Judah?

The answer goes back to his father Ahaz, the wicked king who ruled before him. Ahaz was facing sure destruction from Rezin, king of Syria, and Pekah, the king of Israel, but instead of calling upon the Lord for help, he hired the king of Assyria to pull them off him. In gratitude, Ahaz took a trip to Damascus to meet him and, I guess, to thank him for his help.

While he was there, he saw a pagan altar that impressed him so much that he sent the design back to Uzziah the high priest to have one made just like it. It must have been really nice and shiny because he set aside the Brazen Altar that was before the House of the Lord and replaced it with this new modern version. He instructed the High Priest that all the offerings and sacrifices would now be done on this shiny, new modern altar, but had the audacity to say that when he wanted to inquire of the Lord, he would go over and use the old Brazen Altar that now sat on the north side of the Temple. He discarded the established way the Lord had set down to initiate a new, modern way that was based on pagan worship.

Sounds crazy, right? But have we not done the same thing in dismissing that old-fashioned Gospel of the fear of the Lord for a new and gentler modern Gospel of peace, love and prosperity? Did not Jeremiah cry out, *"... ask for the old paths, where is the good way, and walk therein, and ye shall find rest for your souls. But they said, we will not walk therein."* (Jeremiah 6:16)

I'm sure Ahaz had plenty of justifications. After all, it was Solomon's design, wasn't it? So what's the harm in upgrading it a little bit? Besides, the Brazen Altar was getting old and burnt around the edges and probably needed some touch ups and a new paint job. This new one was bright and shiny. And yeah, it was patterned after a pagan altar, but it's not like he was going to offer up his children on it as a burnt sacrifice. So, what was the problem?

When we operate outside the fear of the Lord, we set the stage for our own judgment. Isaiah's resulting pronouncement against Judah came to fruition, not in Ahaz's generation, but in his son's. Hezekiah felt the full impact of Ahaz's foolishness and had it not been for his extraordinary righteousness before God, Jerusalem would have no doubt been overwhelmed.

Many times, in the Bible when the great stone wheel of judgment would begin to roll because of their sins, God would raise up a solitary man to stand in the gap for His people -- Noah, Joseph, Elijah, Gideon, and many of the judges. Hezekiah was just such a man to stop the full brunt of his father's sins so that the seed would be preserved to bring humanity to the ultimate of saviors, God Himself in the form of His Son Jesus Christ.

Mercy is not free; neither is it cheap. And although God delights in mercy, He is first and foremost a righteous God and there is a price to pay for sin in the form of judgment. If we, as a people, ignore the warnings against a lighter version of the Gospel, all the while making excuses and justifications for our shiny new altar, we will face the same results our fathers have faced. Let us pray that God will raise up unto us a way for repentance to stave off the results of our lack of the fear of God.

> *"O Israel, thy prophets are like the foxes in the deserts.*
>
> *Ye have not gone up into the gaps, neither made up the hedge for the house of Israel to stand in the battle in the day of the LORD.*
>
> *They have seen vanity and lying divination, saying, The LORD saith: and the LORD hath not sent them: and they have made others to hope that they would confirm the word."*
>
> *(Ezekiel 13:4-6)*

All Dogs Go to Heaven

Everybody I know is going to Heaven. (Let me think for a minute … yep, everybody). From the Alpha+ personalities that charge ahead in their own self-righteousness to the casual believers who relax in their own languid reassurance that all is cool with the "Man Upstairs". The only folks I know who say they're not going to Heaven are the ones who don't believe in Heaven anyway! Well, I guess that just makes everything convenient then. We can all relax and be raptured.

But somewhere there is a line.

If everybody is right, then nobody is wrong; and if everybody else is wrong, what makes you think you are right? Peter said that he knew and was sure that Jesus was the Christ. That's all fine, but it's not God who I am wondering about -- I trust God. It's me I don't trust.

A guy named Howard Pitman had an experience years ago when he died in an ambulance and went up before God. God showed him the Day of Judgment where he saw billions of people going up before God to be judged. Multitudes were shot down into Hell like showers of sparks. Some souls went up to Heaven, but nowhere near as many as those who went to Hell. But every once in a while, there would be one who would come up before God and there would be a pause … and then they would be shot down into Hell. He said that when he asked who they were, God replied that those were the self-righteous who thought they were supposed to go to Heaven and stood there justifying themselves to God.

It's been years since I listened to that vision, but that one scene has never left me. It lines up with the admonition Jesus gave us of the broad and narrow paths. ("Lord, Lord, have we not prophesied in your name and in your name done many wonderful works?") While we may all have our own perspective of what is required to get to Heaven, only one perspective matters – and that would His.

Let us be careful that we don't make ourselves to be so squeaky clean that we become Pharisees, or to become so "spiritual" that we think that going out and looking at the trees is a religious experience with God. Some will echo the old assertion of "I don't smoke, and I don't chew, and I don't go with them that do", all the while completely stagnant in their lack of mercy for others. Others will float around in their spiritual effervescence, dispensing "feel good" prophesies laced with sweetness and sugar plums so that everyone will know they are "loved" but leave them clueless as to the holiness that God demands.

There is a walk in the Spirit that found in

neither of these extremes nor anywhere in between them. It is a completely different path, a different perspective, with an entirely different goal. It is a place of surrender before God where you no longer matter. It is being as porous as an open window so that the Spirit of God can pass through you to shower the true mercy of God on others. You will never gain that place in God through your own efforts or spirituality – only through surrender.

Peeking Past the Veil

I read a chapter of Proverbs every day. Whatever today's date is, that's the chapter I read, and there's always something in there for me that day. The one that stopped me today was Proverbs 16:4 – *"The Lord hath made all things for himself: yea, even the wicked for the day of evil."*

Wow. What is <u>that</u> supposed to mean? There's another scripture in Isaiah 45:7 that says,

> *"I form the light, and create darkness: I make peace, and create evil: I the LORD do all these things."*

There are some other Scriptures in the Bible that can really scramble your theologies about the nature of God if you stop and think about them.

Now, I'm not a genius but I'm smart enough to realize how stupid we are. There are a whole lot of things that I don't think we will ever grasp in their entirety until we get to the other side. As Paul said in 1 Corinthians 13, it is as if we are looking through a glass darkly – we can't see clearly – but when we die, we will see things the way they really are. Isaiah said it even better when he said,

> *"And he will destroy in this mountain the face of the covering cast over all people, and the veil that is spread over all nations."* (Isaiah 25:7).

There is a veil over our eyes, a covering that keeps us from seeing things the way they really are in the scope of Eternity.

(Sigh) It seems like the more I learn, the less I understand. But Voltaire once said that to know that you know what you know, and that you don't know what you don't know is wisdom. Yeah, I get it. We really don't know, do we. We just think we know.

But one thing I do know is that God is really real – not just as a theological idea or a point of belief or doctrine to be argued over, but real, as in <u>more</u> real than real. I've had a lot of supernatural experiences with God, and I know a lot of other people who have also. Maybe not everybody gets to hear God speak out of the heavens, but it does happen. And it is not all that uncommon. And then there are visions, instant healings, and other sorts of miracles. I've seen all this stuff with my own eyes. And I have heard Him speak to me. I would never have believed if I hadn't.

But I get a little reticent when speaking about this stuff because a lot of people have not experienced things like that and I'm always afraid they will start looking at me like I am weird if I mention them. As if to say, "You know, he's really a nice guy, but he's just a little bit nuts." Sorry, but why should I be afraid to mention these things? I mean, I didn't do them to myself, and by golly, there's a lot of other people that have had the same experiences, so why, as Paul once said, should it seem a thing incredible? If God can raise the dead, why can't He speak?

All I know is that God really is real. He's there. And no, I don't understand how or why God created evil ... but He says He did, and that's good enough for me. It says in that same chapter of Proverbs that the highway of the upright is to depart from evil and that he that keeps his way preserves his soul. I guess that's all I really need to know.

> *"And unto man he said, Behold, the fear of the Lord, that is wisdom; and to depart from evil is understanding. (Job 28:28)*

New Clothes

"...and His truth endureth to all generations." Psalm 100:5

Think of that! We get to have the same Truth that Adam had, and Noah, and Abraham, and even the Apostle Paul. The very same Truth!

But we live in a world today that feels that "the times they are a-changing". How we look at what is right and what is wrong is relative to new sets of morals. That may be OK for Bob Dylan, but it doesn't work for God.

I believe that the problem started when Satan entered the Bible Colleges – not as a student like everybody else, but as one of the professors. Let me take that back – not as a professor, but as the chairman of the Board.

Once Satan was in charge, the fiery edge of the Gospel was diluted to be more "socially conciliatory". No more "hellfire and brimstone"; no more trembling fear of God; no more judgment for human sin and failings. Everything is relative, and we now have an 11th Commandment – "Thou shalt not offend anyone".

It's a simple formula. Change the personality of God, and guess what? You get a new modern Gospel – one that is kinder and gentler and more loving and inclusive to bring more people into "God's Love". They tried the same thing at the foot of Mount Sinai when Moses went up the mountain.

God is wearing new clothes these days. Yep. He has changed out of those old white robes and has put on some new fashionable digs. They probably have him dressed out in bell-bottom jeans and a T-shirt. In some cases, they've even traded in His old clothes for a dress! I've heard that He may even be a She.

With all this confusion, is it a long stretch to believe that Jesus Christ was a homosexual? Believe it or not, there are those who believe that. So, I guess it's OK to have homosexual Bishops. It all falls into their definition of "God is Love".

Am I dreaming, or am I living in a world of idiots? What, you can't read? The Love of God is not some warm, fuzzy emotion – it's the keeping of God's commandments. At least that's what God says. And since He wrote the Book, I'll go along with Him.

Ah, but there's the rub, isn't it? We don't read the Bible anymore. We listen to our new, modern-age preachers who tell us all the new stuff they've learned. We watch TBN that tells us that everything is love. We study Christian self-help books as if they have the answers to Life. We are now embracive of all religions because, after all, we all worship the same God. As for that old-fashioned King James

Bible, well, it's a simple stretch to re-phase it to change the words that we don't like, and if necessary, even omit whole passages. And we'll call it an International version to make it seem easier and more in tune with our new world that we have built.

And you wonder why our church world has lost its power in God? Then again, maybe you don't wonder because it's been so long since you've experienced a real outpouring of the Holy Ghost that you don't even know the difference anymore.

That same Bible that we've relegated to a dusty bookshelf warned us that these days would come, and here they are. And it will get a lot worse before it gets better. Soon, they'll be hunting down anyone that holds to the original precepts of the Bible and will kill them thinking they're doing God service. Standing against sin will be considered a "hate crime" and preaching repentance will leave you open to lawsuits for hurting people's feelings. Saying that Jesus Christ is the only name under heaven by which a man can be saved will be deemed intolerant, judgmental, and divisive – a crime against humanity.

The Word of God is not a textbook or a novel. It is the very Bread of Life, and without it, you will never be able to see through the subtle deceptions that are coming upon the face of the earth. It is Light, and if you don't read it, you can't see. It is Life, and if you don't eat it, you will die. It is Truth, and without it, you are in a lie.

The Word of God will not change, no matter how they try to "improve" it. The Truth will endure throughout Eternity, and I, for one, will never compromise it. I will not back down, back up, or give in. I will stand for it because it is the only truth upon the face of the earth, and it will never change.

I'm not interested in being "nice", and neither were the prophets of God. I'm interested in being right with God.

I'm not worried about hurting anyone's feelings. They will hurt a lot more if they end up in Hell.

I'm not interested in being socially or religiously "correct". I'm interested in the Truth.

I don't want to be part of the majority. Only a few will choose the narrow path that leads to Heaven.

A revival is coming, folks, but it is not coming through the established church world. It is going to come through a fierce people set in battle array that will not break their ranks and will not surrender to a changing world (Joel 2:1-11). You may not recognize them because they won't look like your polished, theological seminary graduates.

They'll look like John the Baptist -- and he had his head cut off for preaching the truth.

> *"And unto man he said, Behold, the fear of the Lord, that is wisdom; and to depart from evil is understanding."* Job 28:28

Baskin Robbins

When I was a kid, I used to love to go to the local Baskin Robbins Ice Cream Store. They had 31 flavors! I would always be looking for the latest exotic flavor to try – Pistachio Almond, Blueberry Cheesecake, Cherries Jubilee, Peanut Butter 'n Chocolate, and on and on. There was always something new to try. My kids, on the other hand, always want Vanilla, Chocolate, or Strawberry. Man, that just sounds so dull to me, but that's what they like. So, when Mom brings home ice cream, she always gets one of the basic flavors for them and something crazy for me.

I have found that Life is a lot like that. God created 31 different flavors, and not everybody likes Rocky Road or Mint Chocolate Chip. Some of us just like plain Vanilla. And if there was no vanilla, how could you make a Banana Split? I may lead my life a little on the left side of crazy but thank God not everyone is like that. If everyone were like me, then there would be no Baskin Robbins!

I love being saved and I love being in the Spirit, but sometimes in my exuberance I get so intense that I tend to roll over others in my excitement and forget that some people like Vanilla, not Nutty Cream Cheese Brownie. Everybody has a different flavor.

The Bible says in 1st Corinthians 12 that God

has created us all for a different role and has placed us all in the Body in different places for different functions so that the Body will be able to do what God intended for it.

In other words, God likes Baskin Robbins!

We all have different gifts, and Paul said in that same chapter to covet earnestly the best gifts – yes, it's okay to want to do exciting things – but there is yet a more excellent way ... and then Paul launches into that great chapter on Charity, 1st Corinthians 13 – one of the greatest chapters in the whole Bible.

What good would it be to have the fanciest ice cream in the world if you forgot the whole purpose for what God intended for the Church and for you? While we may all like different flavors of ice cream, one thing is important, and that is Charity. The Gospel of Jesus Christ is about others.

Not everyone is called to go to exotic lands, but everyone is called to pray. And that is where the real calling of God is established. If the battles have not been won on our knees, they will not be won out on the streets. The real battlefield is the prayer room.

When we forget this, some other exotic ice cream may look good, but it will taste terrible.

The Lost Art of Prayer

> *"Hear ye now what the LORD saith; Arise, contend thou before the mountains, and let the hills hear thy voice."* (Micah 6:1)

Somewhere in the modern development of our churches we have lost the art of prayer. We've lost it so badly that we don't even realize that we've lost it.

Fifty years ago, we didn't pray like we do today – we prayed like warriors. The prayer room was a place of contending and battle where you went in there to wage spiritual warfare as you fought your way up to the Throne of God. You knew going in that Satan would withstand you and do his best to hinder your prayers, make you weary, and convince you to quit before you won the victory. Prayer, real contending prayer, was work, a labor of love in the furnace room of war. You went in, not to sing songs and feel happy, but to fight for the cause, to contend for deliverance from the powers of darkness, and stand for the glory and honor of God.

The prayer warriors of those days talked about "praying it through". You didn't stop when you felt like it – you prayed it all the way through until you got the victory. If that meant all night, then you prayed all night. Why would you quit before you got your answer?

But oh, when you did! What an incredible

rush of glory when you broke through! It would feel like the heavens opened up and sunshine and glory would pour down. When you got your answer, it was as sure and solid as the foundations of the Earth. You knew you had touched the Throne of God. It was always worth the fight.

Today, when I speak about storming the Throne of God in prayer, I get quizzical or blank looks from those listening to me. The response I get back is that God is our "Daddy" and because He loves us so, we shouldn't have to struggle to gain access to Him in prayer.

Is that really faith though? Or is it a form of presumption? Do we assume that because we believe in Jesus, we merely have to mention our desires and God will leap to our call? We simply guess that if we whisper our thoughts to God, somehow, He will answer … we hope. We pay no price because there is no battle. The problem is, however, that neither is there any victory.

But if you want to call for the heavens to pour out the rain like Elijah did, then you have to pray like Elijah did. There is nothing free in God – nothing. Elijah was a man who stood in the awesome fear of Almighty God, but because he stood in that righteousness, he was also able to stand in that holy boldness that only comes from the fear of the Lord.

Proverbs is definitive in its statement that in the fear of the Lord is great confidence. You cannot approach the holiness of God in blood-washed victory if there is the slightest shadow of sin in your life. But even in that righteousness, Elijah was a man who knew that he had to contend before the Almighty in fervent effectual prayer if he wanted to see God rend the heavens. He was a warrior in God because that's what it took to move the heavenlies.

It is said that prayer moves God. And great moves require great prayer. And that takes great faith, not a faith that merely hopes God will answer, but a faith that stakes its claim on the rights that were purchased by the Blood of Jesus Christ and refuses to give in until the victory is won.

But the power to pray like that does not come overnight nor is it as simple as flipping on a light switch. There is a process that starts with the Word of God and journeys through valleys of faith to strip us of our fleshly ways and brings us through spiritual depths that are never realized nor suspected by casual Christianity. It is a place of the Cross -- a place of blood, suffering, and death and of our ultimate rest in God.

It is a place where warriors are forged, where prayers are answered, and where great moves of God are birthed.

Maybe

> *"He that dwelleth in the secret place of the most High shall abide under the shadow of the Almighty." (Psalms 91:1)*

Sometimes I wonder if very many people really understand prayer. It seems that it is becoming more of a function like brushing your teeth than a source of life, and like brushing your teeth, it has become something we do (or as least say we do) because we are supposed to, rather than it being a desperate necessity of life itself. We have lost the art of prayer, and in so doing, have lost touch with God.

Instead of entering into that deep chamber of personal prayer in the presence of the Most Holy, we have learned to pray <u>at</u> God, supposing that if we lay out our request list on the table, maybe He will read it. I listen to church members as they take turns praying, each making his or her little speech, going down the checklist of the items that need to be addressed. I suppose we figure that if we pop the words out there, somehow, they will make their way up through the airways and clouds and grab His attention. Or maybe someone up there gathers them all up and brings them to Him. Maybe He will listen; maybe He won't. After all, there's a lot of stuff going on up there and He must be pretty busy.

Or maybe it's just a simple numbers game. We get on Facebook and round up as many Likes as we can. Maybe if we can get enough people posting those little praying hands, surely, He will pay attention. So, we tell everyone to pray, and of course, everyone says they will – and some really do – but you wonder at what level of intensity do they take that request to the Throne of God. Are we talking about "contending prayer" or a 60-second snapshot?

I don't want to sound critical or ugly here, but I am not seeing what the old-timers used to call "storming the Throne of God", crashing the gates of Heaven, or shaking the Throne of God until He answers. They used to call it "praying it through". Does anyone do that anymore? Or are we simply satisfied with crumbs? Do we merely hope that somehow maybe, just maybe, God will answer our prayers, but we don't have what it takes to make sure?

Later in Psalm 91, David says that all these promises are realized because you have made God "your habitation". This is not tossing up some grocery lists of prayer requests in His general direction, hoping that something will stick, or assume that if we speak the word, God will answer because some vague scripture you read says so. That is not faith; that is presumption.

No, what David is describing is a deep

personal relationship with God that pierces the veil and puts you right into the presence of God. You are there. You are not only standing right in His presence but have entered into that "secret place of the Most High". It's you and Him. Together. You can feel His presence. There is a hush of holiness that fills the room. He has become your habitation and you abide in Him and He in you. This is beyond faith. You have stepped into the reality of Eternity. Now you can ask what you will, and He will answer you. There is no question, no wondering. You don't have to quote a scripture to bolster your faith – you were there, standing right before Him in that secret place! You have gotten the victory and it is done!

I have said that revivals have to be prayed in. There is no other way because it is prayer that moves God. The same applies to our personal lives and the life of our churches. Many churches these days have no prayer room, and their prayer meetings attract only 1% of the congregation. And when they do gather to pray, it never reflects the same intensity that I have described here. They are not desperate for God, and when you listen to them pray, you can hear the absence of it. They just don't get it. They acknowledge it; they hear, but they don't hearken.

I am sure many of you will quickly jump to a defense of other methods of prayer. Yes, God can hear the faintest cry of the heart. Yes, He knows every word that you speak. Yes, everybody is different in their approach to God. Yes, yes, yes. I have heard it all. But I would ask you, if faint-hearted prayers and anemic prayer meetings are so valid, then where are the results? As Gideon said, "Where are the miracles that our fathers told us about?" Where are the outpourings of the Holy Ghost that crash out of the sky and lay you flat? Where are the altars packed with souls coming to salvation? Where are the manifestations of power in casting out demons? Where are the healings? Not the hope that God will slowly ooze healing into them or guide the surgeon's hands, but the supernatural, right now, in your face, power of God, instantaneous power of healing? Where are the prayer hours that are so supernatural that you get lost in them?

Do you believe God or not? If these signs will follow them that believe, where are they? Maybe we do not realize how desperate we are. Maybe we have traded that secret place of the Most High for a place of convenience. Maybe we have not seen an example of what a real prayer warrior prays like. Maybe we have lost the art of prayer.

Maybe we care.

Maybe we don't.

Jonah and Miracles

When ministering to a church recently, I prayed for God to manifest a miracle of healing right in their midst so that this church could really see and believe. These were good-hearted people who honestly wanted to hear what I had to say and, in some cases, hung on every word I spoke. They believed me about the abundance of miracles that I had experienced in Africa; they applauded all the wonderful things that had been done and the souls that had been saved; they even hungered for the marvelous outpouring of the Spirit that had been poured down on the services over there … they just couldn't seem to take that extra step of faith off the edge of that secure religious cliff they were on and have enough blind trust to fall off into the invisible hands of God.

It is a difficult thing to trust your life to something you can't see.

So, I prayed for God to manifest a supernatural miracle right before their eyes so they could see. Sounded like a good idea to me. But when I took it to prayer, the Lord answered me back with,

> *"An evil and adulterous generation seeketh after a sign; and there shall no sign be given to it, but the sign of the prophet Jonas" (Matthew 12:39)*

Yikes! Kind of harsh, aren't you, Lord? But I

remembered back to when the Lord spoke to me several years ago when I was praying for the churches and trying to explain to the Lord that they were really nice people. His answer to me was, "I will spue the lukewarm out of my mouth … and you think they're *nice*?" Oops.

If they were so "nice", why weren't they cut to the heart for the lost? Where was the fire? Where was the kind of zeal that had eaten them up? Where was their brokenness at the altar of prayer? If they were so "nice", why were they so complacent and lackadaisical? Why were they so much like the Church of Laodicea in Revelations?

I thought back to the rich man and Lazarus. The message there was that we have the Word of God, but if we won't hear the Word of God, we wouldn't listen to someone even if they came back from the dead. Nineveh repented at the preaching of Jonah, but how many of us have forsaken our ways that are so cemented in this world to take up a challenge of ferocious faith to hold up the Blood-Stained Banner? Oh, we say we do … and then we make excuses of why we do not.

It is not miracles that we need to see, but the reproof of the Word of God. Proverbs 1:23 encourages us:

"Turn you at my reproof: behold, I will pour out my spirit unto you, I will make known my words unto you." (Proverbs 1:23)

But hey, we read what we want and believe what we choose, and that, more than anything else, determines our level of faith. We determine our own level of faith. Miracles won't do it.

The Obadiah Church

> *"And Elijah the Tishbite, who was of the inhabitants of Gilead, said unto Ahab, As the LORD God of Israel liveth, before whom I stand, there shall not be dew nor rain these years, but according to my word.*
> *(1 Kings 17:1)*

A reflection of the last days can be seen in this chapter in Elijah's life. Israel had forsaken the true faith of their fathers for an idolatrous religion that was pressed upon them by Ahab's marriage to Jezebel – a satanic union of church and state. The land seemed to flourish in prosperity that was undoubtedly attributed to this new religion of Baal. Baal, of course, is the god of love who preaches a kinder, gentler gospel message than that old, stern and judgmental Jehovah and is more in tune with the pleasures of the world. Satan's job is not to try to convince us that sin is not sin, but rather that we can get away with sin because God will always forgive us, understand our human failings, and cover our sin with His love. That is the god of Baal, and that is precisely why the people loved Baal and hated the prophets of God.

How like today! We have a form of godliness, but we have denied the power thereof because we have pulled away from the holiness and fear of God that our grandfathers preached to us. We denigrate the old Brush Arbor revivals, and then wonder why the modern church is so anemic. But although we are disenchanted with the old message, we still adhere to the idea of Jesus … we just manufactured it into a different form that has an uncanny resemblance to the golden calves at the foot of Mt. Sinai.

Elijah was chased to the Brook Cherith to be fed by the ravens until the brook dried up. Every morning and every evening the birds came to sustain him. I'm not sure how Elijah felt about being fed these delicacies from birds, but this is certainly not the same picture that we see in how today's ecclesiastical royalty is being served. But then, neither are they the type of preachers that we would expect to march into Ahab's throne room and tell him that he is going to Hell.

When there was no sustenance left in Israel, Elijah was sent out of the country to Zidon. When there is no more movement of the Holy Spirit in the Church, God will start moving outside it. Elijah meets a widow at the gate of the city. Why the gate and not the well or somewhere nondescript? I don't know, but the gate of the city was always the place of authority and judgment. Perhaps there is a message there, but at any rate, he sends her off to make him a cake with a pronouncement from God that He will sustain them … not lavishly, perhaps, but God <u>will</u>

sustain them for 3-1/2 years.

This is a picture of the church in the last days – a shell of her former self, outside the denominational structure, in the shadow of the Jezebel Whore of Revelations, with just enough of the meal of the Word of God and the oil of the Spirit to sustain herself through this time of spiritual famine. One day at a time. There was only enough for them to be sustained by the faith that God would keep them for one more day. I don't know how bad the end times will be, but both Jesus and Daniel said that it would be worse than anything the world has seen since the beginning of time. That seems to match the picture we see here in Zarephath.

> *"Come, my people, enter thou into thy chambers, and shut thy doors about thee: hide thyself as it were for a little moment, until the indignation be overpast. For, behold, the LORD cometh out of his place to punish the inhabitants of the earth for their iniquity..." (Isaiah 26:20-21)*

When the day of reckoning finally came, Elijah was sent to Obadiah to call Ahab. God could have sent him directly to Ahab, but He didn't. He used Obadiah. In Obadiah, we see a picture of yet another church in the last days, but we don't see an oppressed church like the one of the Widow of Zarephath, but a worldly church that is still attached to the kingdom of this world. Yes, Obadiah hid the prophets from Jezebel's wrath, but he never disassociated himself from Ahab. Out of his own mouth, he confessed that Ahab was still his lord. Here is the compromised church, hanging onto her love for prosperity and comfort. She is not willing to stand up and challenge the sin and unrighteousness of the worldly system that she is part of, and not willing to leave it for the scarcities of the desert. It is this Obadiah that God chooses to engage in this last great challenge between the prophet and the king.

The story of Mount Carmel is rich with imagery – the water, the fire, the judgment, and the sound of abundance of rain, all of which would be better served in another article – but it is the picture of the two churches that concerns me here. I hear talk of the "triumphant church", of the great things to come, and how we will move into the greatest Church Age that we have ever seen. I have even heard that the wealth of the sinners will be laid up for the just and thereby transferred to us, and we will get rich. Why do we so desperately hang on to this? Is it because we can no longer see the world for what it really is? Have we become an Obadiah church, touting our "good works" as an excuse for our compromise with the world, and in doing so have aligned ourselves with Ahab, even calling him lord and are unwilling to make a stand for truth and righteousness?

Perhaps God, in His incredible mercy, will allow the Church to be engaged again in the last showdown between the Spirit of Elijah and the Church of Baal. Not all is well with the Church, nor will it ever be as long as we retain our worldliness and refrain from reproving the world of its sin. There will be some hard choices to be made which the Church may not have the strength and integrity to make. When Elijah stood alone on top of Mount Carmel, where was Obadiah? Do we fear, as did Obadiah, to confront the world and take a stand against a false religion of love, peace, and prosperity in the face of lust, sin, and covetousness?

God in His mercy may yet engage the Church in these last days, but I believe she will be sifted with the "sieve of vanity" as Isaiah warns us in chapter 30:28. The choices she will face will not only be hard, but they will seem radical and extreme. It will be a solitary stand against that which seems to be normal, but it is a choice that she will have to make, nonetheless.

Kosmos

One of the recurring issues I hear about is that the Old Covenant is still valid. The point is made that Jesus said that He didn't come to destroy the Law but to fulfill it, and that until Heaven and Earth pass, not a jot or tittle would pass from the Law until all be fulfilled. How would that be possible if the Old Covenant is done away with?

The other day I was reading Colossians slowly, trying to absorb each thought Paul was delivering. I came to the passage about legalism in Colossians 2:16-23, and I stopped in my tracks –

> *"Let no man therefore judge you in meat, or in drink, or in respect of a holy day, or of the new moon, or of the sabbath days: Which are a shadow of things to come; but the body is of Christ.*
>
> *Let no man beguile you of your reward in a voluntary humility and worshipping of angels, intruding into those things which he hath not seen, vainly puffed up by his fleshly mind,*
>
> *And not holding the Head, from which all the body by joints and bands having nourishment ministered, and knit together, increaseth with the increase of God.*
>
> *Wherefore if ye be dead with Christ from the rudiments of the world, why, as though living in the world, are ye subject to ordinances,*

(Touch not; taste not; handle not; Which all are to perish with the using;) after the commandments and doctrines of men?

Which things have indeed a show of wisdom in will worship, and humility, and neglecting of the body; not in any honor to the satisfying of the flesh. "

The first word that I was curious about was "rudiments". In the Greek, it is "*stoicheion*", which means to put or to go in a row, as in a series. Basically, it means the primary principles that other things are based on … or in a word, the rudimentary elements. Paul is in a discussion here about the Old Law, so it is obvious that these "rudiments of the world" are pointing to the carnal ceremonial elements of the Mosaic Law. Okay, I don't want to get over-complicated here – this is just about the carnal ordinances of the Law – I got it.

The next word that reached out and grabbed me was "the world". This word is *Kosmos* (or Cosmos for all you Carl Sagan fans). This is an interesting word in that it means that which pertains to space, the sum total of the material universe, all the beauty in it, and all the persons … but not time! Are you with me so far? This is huge! Not time!

If I am reading this passage from Colossians correctly, Paul is saying that all the carnal ordinances that constitute the covenant of death are not supposed to affect us anymore because we are no longer in the Kosmos. We are outside time! When we received Eternal Life, something more than a warm feeling happened to us – our soul transcended the dimension of Time. The Law hasn't passed away – it's still valid in the carnal world and will never pass away and it still stands as a testament of judgment against all flesh – but we are no longer part of that world. We are dead with Christ from the rudiments of the world, we don't live in that old system, and so therefore we are no longer subject to those old ordinances that Christ disavowed when He nailed them to His Cross.

Wow. I was stunned. When we accepted Jesus Christ as our personal Savior, we passed from death unto life and left behind the ordinances of touch not, taste not, handle not. We no longer have to put the blood of bulls and goats on our right ear, our right thumb, and our right toe. We don't have to keep the dietary laws or the festivals that foreshadowed Christ and the New Testament. We don't have to deal with the sacrifices of dead animals.

The Old Law is still there and still valid as a condemnation to all who live in the Kosmos, but we left that world when we got saved! We are no longer creatures of Time. We are free.

Isaiah 58 – the Key to Revival

> *Be ye ashamed, O ye husbandmen; howl, O ye vinedressers, for the wheat and for the barley; because the harvest of the field is perished. (Joel 1:11)*

A prominent church leader asked me to bring a message on revival to a conference of church leaders in Nigeria because although they had been fasting and praying and crying out to God for revival, nothing was working. Something was wrong, and they wanted to know what it was.

I have heard many pastors say that they have tried everything they can think of to spark a move of God in their church, but nothing seems to work. It is because they are missing the key.

The scripture in Joel 1:11 is one of the most damning indictments there is against the Church. God tells us to be ashamed because the harvest has perished. And God blames us. We are the husbandmen, the ones who are responsible for the harvest and the souls that have been lost. All the curses, drought, and famine that we see in the first chapter of Joel that have fallen upon the Church are a direct result of our failure to go out and win souls.

This is the key. If we fix this, we can begin to see a restoration of the wheat, the wine, and the oil, the meat offering and drink offering, the joy and blessings – all the things of the Spirit of God that He has taken away from us. If we do not, all the tears and crying out to God will not work. It is not the hearers of the Word that are justified; it is the doers (Romans 2:13).

Isaiah 58 gives us a clear picture of what we have to do. The chapter starts with the Lord admonishing his prophet to cry aloud to the Church and tell her what her transgression is. Somebody has to speak up and say something or the Church will continue to wander around clueless as to what is wrong.

He goes on to say that the Church complains that they are seeking God daily, they delight in His ways, they have kept the commandments, and have fasted and afflicted their souls … but they get no answer from God.

Why isn't God answering? This is the same cry we hear from across the ecclesiastical landscape today. Why are our churches so dead? What do we need to do to revive them? The Church thinks they are doing everything they are supposed to do, but nothing seems to be working.

The Lord challenges us right from the beginning of the chapter with some pointed questions:

- What is it you are fasting for? Is it for you or others?
- Have you sought to loosen the bands of wickedness and undo the heavy burdens by bringing them to Salvation?
- Have you let the oppressed go free and broken the yoke of sin by bringing the Gospel to them?
- Have you dealt your bread, the Bread of Life, to the hungry?
- Have you brought the poor into your house, the House of God?
- When you saw the naked, did you cover them with the robes of righteousness?

Have you? Because verse 8 says that if you would do these things, your light would break forth as the morning, your health would spring forth speedily, your righteousness would go before you, and the Lord would be your guard to protect you. The Spirit of the Lord would shine off you and would encompass you.

Not only that, but the next verse says that when you call, the Lord shall answer. Did you catch that? Not maybe, not sometimes … SHALL answer. And when you cry, He would say, "Here I am". You want answers from God? Here are His instructions and promises to you. Here you have a clear route to true honor from God. Honor is not some title or position in the Church – honor, true honor, is when the Lord hears your prayers and answers them. That is honor! And you get that by showing mercy on the lost.

But there is more …

He says in verse 10 that if you draw out your soul to the hungry and satisfy the afflicted soul – and you do that by feeding them the Word of God -- then your light will rise in obscurity and your darkness will be as the noon day. He will not only lift you up and honor you, but you will shine with the glory of God.

He says He will guide you continually – Oh, to be always led by the Spirit of God! – and He will satisfy your soul in drought and make your bones fat. Even in the time of spiritual famine, you will be like a tree planted by the Living Waters. Why? Because you took it upon yourself to carry out His Great Commission to reach out to the lost.

But here is the best part of this passage – if you will shoulder this burden, God says that those who come forth of you, your spiritual offspring, will build the old waste places and raise up the foundations of many generations. Remember Nehemiah viewing the waste places of Jerusalem, a picture of the spiritual desolation of the Church? That's what revival is about, to build those old waste places and restore the Church to its proper place and glory in God. If you will go out and win souls and have mercy on the lost, those whom you win to the Lord will rebuild the old broken-down foundations of the Church and will rebuild it in the way it should be.

But here is the greatest honor -- you will be called the restorer of paths to dwell in. I can think of no greater honor than to be called by God to restore the paths for the Church to walk in. In Eternity, will you have that honor bestowed on you, that you are one of the restorers who built the old waste places of the Church and broke through the spiritual desolation to bring the fires of revival back to the Church?

Or will you be one of those who heard the call, but never made the decision to stand up and answer it?

Sin and Prayer

> *"... and he that owneth the house shall come and tell the priest, saying, It seemeth to me there is as it were a plague in the house: Then the priest shall command that they empty the house, before the priest go into it to see the plague, that all that is in the house be not made unclean: and afterward the priest shall go in to see the house" (Leviticus 14:35-36)*

When there was leprosy found in a house, everything inside that house was to be removed while the walls were scraped and cleansed. If that didn't work, they yanked the stones that were affected and scraped the walls and took the dust and stones away to an unclean place outside the city. It doesn't say what was meant by an "unclean place", but I get the impression it would have been like a place where you dump your septic tank.

If the priest came back in seven days and the leprosy was still not purged, then the whole house was to be dumped out there in the dung pit. Anything that was left in the house had to be taken and dumped there also. The leprosy would have infected everything that was still in the house.

The laws for leprosy in a house also apply to churches. If we allow the least amount of sin to enter in, it will grow like cancer and corrupt the entire house and those who remain in it.

But Satan never comes with a big brass band. He always enters in with subtlety and a smooth, satanic grace. He may start with just a touch of worldliness in the song service, or a relaxation of dress codes, or maybe just a broader acceptance of other ideas. It always seems so harmless at first …

Satan's ultimate objective isn't to make you think that sin is not sin; Satan's job is to make you think you can get away with sin. To do that, he must reduce the threat of sin, make it more palatable, excusable, and forgivable. His lie to Eve in the Garden is still used today, "Thou shalt not surely die."

At a recent Bible Study, I listened to a well-meaning and fervent believer make the case that even if you are in sin, God will still hear your prayers. He argued in a deeply theological bent and drew from wells of scholasticism and theory and thought, but the basic argument was a defense of sin.

You cannot minimize sin. Neither can you excuse it, justify it, or rationalize it away. God hates sin. He had to watch His only begotten Son be tortured and slaughtered like an animal to cover your filth, degeneracy, and rebellion … and you would have the audacity to go to His Throne in prayer covered in this filth?

The root cause of this kind of entrance into the Church today rests in our resistance to the preaching of the real, chilling fear of God. Everything is about love these days, while the preaching about the fear of God is considered caustic, legalistic, and harsh. But when you lose your fear of God, you lose your power in God. And as a result, sin creeps in every so slowly. Soon, sin does not seem so bad.

And we wonder why our churches are so anemic.

Choice of Faith

> *"Now faith is the substance of things hoped for, the evidence of things not seen." (Hebrews 11:1)*

Faith is a choice. It is not something that is thrust upon you or presented as a set of choices to pick from. It is something that you have to reach for that lies beyond the grasp of your understanding. You have to choose to believe.

I have always been struck by the passage in 2nd Thessalonians 2:11 that tells us that God will send strong delusion to those who do not have a love of the truth but have pleasure in unrighteousness. This life, therefore, is a test for our souls. We are eternal creatures created in His likeness, but our choices determine our final destiny. Will we follow our hearts in a path that leads to self-gratification, or will we choose the fear of the Lord? Only we can make that choice.

Faith, then, is not a matter of believing in God because it makes sense. The Gospel does not make sense to the carnal mind – not the unseen existence of another world, not the path we are called to that leads through the sufferings of the Body of Christ, nor the ultimate victory that was won on the Cross. Everything about God is contrary to the world we live in. And yet, He asks us to close our eyes and believe.

Faith is a choice we make that is born out of hope. We hope in the righteousness of God. We hope that it is true that there really is a God who is holy, that Truth is supreme, that those who hunger and thirst for righteousness shall be filled, and that, in the final culmination of all things, we will walk on streets of glory. We hope, and we make a choice to believe in hope as did Abraham, and we rejoice in hope of the glory of God (Romans 5:2).

Faith that is born out of such hope stretches us past our horizons and creates a vision in our hearts to believe God for the impossible, to take us past what we can see, and reach all the way into Eternity.

Faith is the very substance of that righteousness that we hope for because as we reach through the portal of Eternity, we grab hold of the hem of His garment and touch the Throne of God.

Six Principles

The message of revival that I have been bringing is predicated on the prophecies that are in the Book of Joel, both those about the last great revival that is coming and those about the times leading up to it. But the foundation for the whole message rests upon a base of 6 vital principles of revival. These principles never change. Throughout time, they have been the bedrock foundation that all revivals have been based upon.

The first principle to understand is that revival is not about feeling good, having exciting church services, or receiving wonderful blessings. It's not even about the miracles or the outpouring of the Spirit. Those are the <u>results</u> of revival, not the focus. Revival is about winning souls – first, foremost, and always. The primary reason God sends revival is so that the Church will rise up and shine the Light of Salvation to the millions of lost souls who are on their way to Hell. God is not willing that any should burn in Hell, but He uses His Body to bring that message of hope to them. Jesus said that if He be lifted up, He will draw all men unto Him, and that is what revival is all about. (John 12:32)

The second principle of revival is that the Gospel of Jesus Christ is not about you. The Gospel is about others, others, others. The Church has been flooded with messages that are all about what God can do for you, how Jesus wants to bless His people, and all the blessings and good things that God will give you. It's almost as if all we want to talk about is not how we can serve God, but how He can serve us. Gone are the admonitions about taking upon ourselves the sufferings of the Cross, walking a crucified walk in subjection to His Will, and the call to sacrifice for the Cross.

We have to take our focus off of ourselves and place it on others. This is the very essence of Charity in 1 Corinthians 13. Agape is not just a "love" that is little more than some warm fuzzy emotion; it is love in action, the giving of yourself out of love so that souls can be saved. Jesus died to save sinners, and He calls us to follow Him into that same calling. "Deny thyself, pick up your cross, and follow me." (Matt. 16:24). Until you get your focus off yourself, God cannot use you to bring revival.

The third principle to understand is that there is a price to pay for revival. Nothing in God is free. And the price for revival is high – this is the reason why true Holy Ghost revivals are so rare. You cannot expect to sit in church and wait for God to drop a revival into your waiting lap – it will not happen. At some point, you will have to get up and do something ... but if you do nothing, nothing will happen. God will not send His precious souls to a people who do not care enough to answer the call to battle and fight for them. If you draw nigh unto Him, He will draw nigh unto you (James 4:8). There is a price to pay.

The fourth principle is very like the third in that it insists that revivals have to be prayed in. This is not a light statement. Throughout history, before every revival, you will see the saints laboring in intense prayer, sometimes for years, before God begins to move. And not the light, easy-going "little talks with Jesus", but the ferocious contending before the Throne of God that moves the Almighty. We must be as desperate as Rachael in Genesis 30:1 when, as a barren wife, she cried out to her lord, "Give me children lest I die!" We, in like manner, need to cry out in desperation, "Give us souls, lest we die!" Prayer moves God. If you want a great move of God, it takes great prayer. If you want it to rain, you will have to pray like Elijah.

The fifth principle is that no revival comes without repentance. If the cry for revival is not accompanied by true heart-rending repentance, then nothing will change, and we will remain stuck in the same apostasy that killed the last move of God. Two good examples are in Nehemiah and Daniel. Nehemiah was the king's cupbearer and heard of the desolation of Jerusalem. Before going to the king in supplication to restore the city of God, however, he first fasted and prayed day and night in repentance for the children of Israel. Daniel, likewise, when he read Jeremiah's prophesy that after 70 years, Jerusalem would be restored, did not call his friends to sing and rejoice, but rather, he fell to his knees in repentance for his people. Daniel knew that even though it was written in the Word of God, revival would not come without repentance.

The last principle is a little different than the others. It is not about something we need to do, but rather what God provides for us. I have noticed that every revival is started by someone who has a vision for revival. There is always someone who is lit on fire by a vision that is greater than what he sees around him. He is the lightning that starts the fire. Gideon sought the face of God in secret and would not compromise with the Church that had been taken over by the world, and because of that, the angel told him to go in that strength and he would deliver Israel. Jonathan was willing to climb up the rocks on his hands and knees to take on the enemy, no matter what the odds, because he believed God could deliver them. In every place where you see a picture of God's deliverance and ensuing revival, you will see a man of God who looked beyond his circumstances and believed God for revival. All the other conditions for the fires of revival may be there, but it takes a man or woman with a vision to strike the first match.

Revival is coming, folks. Where it will strike first and how fast the fire will spread is a matter of conjecture, but wherever it strikes, you will find all of the above underlying it.

Old Winebottles

> *"But when they departed from Perga, they came to Antioch in Pisidia, and went into the synagogue on the sabbath day, and sat down.*
>
> *And after the reading of the law and the prophets the rulers of the synagogue sent unto them, saying, Ye men and brethren, if ye have any word of exhortation for the people, say on."* (Acts 13:14-15)

And so, they did.

This formula seemed to have worked fairly well in Cyprus, so why not try it here on the mainland? Pretty much it amounted to run down a quick history of the Messianic story, dismiss the Levitical covenant that these Jews had invested such a huge amount of intense obedience into, explain to them that all they have to do now is believe in the Nazarene, toss out the blood sacrifices, and ask God to forgive them. Pretty simple.

And oh, by the way, if they didn't, they would burn in Hell.

Unfortunately, unlike Sergius Paulus on Cyprus, the response from these Jews was a little less than accommodating. What a surprise. But it was Paul's classic answer that clinched it for them,

> *"For they that dwell at Jerusalem, and their rulers, because they knew him not, nor yet the voices of the prophets which are read every sabbath day, they have fulfilled them in condemning him . . .*
>
> *Beware therefore, lest that come upon you, which is spoken of in the prophets;*
>
> *Behold, ye despisers, and wonder, and perish: for I work a work in your days, a work which ye shall in no wise believe, though a man declare it unto you." (Acts 13:27, 40-41)*

Budda bing, budda bang!

Paul would not have been a good used car salesman, but he certainly made his point – the old religious system was finished, and God was moving in a brand-new direction. Not that God had not given them plenty of notice – the Old Testament is full of distinct and revealing prophecies – it's just that they never saw it.

But it is always that way. The religious rulers had read the voices of the prophets every Sabbath but never heard what they were saying. Why was that? Were they just more comfortable with a religious spirit that had constructed rigid limits? Or were they bent on following their own hearts rather than surrender to the leading of the Spirit of God when it led in ways that they did not like?

Whatever the reason, that same religious tendency to reject any new stirring of the Holy Spirit continues today. Just recently, I spent a few weeks in eastern Congo bringing a message of revival to several churches that were part of a large denomination there. The results were explosive – over 700 souls came to the altar, churches were revitalized to go back out and bring in souls, and a general spirit of rejoicing was ringing in their services for the first time in decades. Pastors told me that it had been years since anyone had gotten saved at their churches, but now they were excited with this new message to bring in the lost and start the wheels of revival rolling.

Guess what happened next. The elders rose up and told these pastors that they were not allowed to do that. In this denomination, you have to be saved for 6 years before you are allowed to witness or minister to others. They warned the pastors that if they continued to send their people out to the streets to bring in the lost, they would kick those pastors out of the denomination.

Huh? Am I hearing this right? This denomination, which had been forged in the fires of its own revival a couple of generations ago, now could not recognize a moving of that same Spirit that had fashioned it years ago.

And the pastor's response? *"We are lit, no more going back, no more fear or worry, we going forward, we are pursuing it. We are determined to see the Congo being revived for change and transformed for God's glory."*

Go get 'em, Pastor! Forget these religious Pharisees who would try to stop a genuine move of the Holy Ghost! Ring the bell of Freedom and declare liberty to the lost. Let every devil in Hell be put on notice that we are not going back to the stifling consort of religious ritualism but are moving forward into a new day of revival.

Think this is unique to the religious Pharisees of Jesus' and Paul's day, or that this is happening in Africa but would never happen here in America? Think again. The Bible is full of warnings to the Church in the last days that there will be a famine for hearing the Word of God (Amos 8:11) and that the people will be starving for pasture and not be able to find it (Joel 1:18). There will be a great falling away (2 Thess. 2:3) in the midst of a swarm of churches who will heap up to themselves the teachers to tell them the things they want to hear (2 Timothy 4:3) and turn their ears away from hearing the truth.

As Pogo warned us, "We have met the enemy, and it is us."

Revival is coming. It is written in the Book of Joel and Isaiah; it shall come to pass. But it is not coming to the churches. Once, when I was wrestling with the Lord in prayer about the church in America, He spoke directly to me in distinct words,

> *"I will give the churches a certain space of time to repent ... and they will not repent. And then I will raise up stones in their place."*

Revival is coming to a new generation of believers who will throw off denominational constraints in favor of a freedom in the Spirit that will lead to a new sense of holiness and righteousness in the fear of Almighty God. God will raise up a Gideon Generation to become the army spoken about in Joel to bring the greatest revival of all time just before Jesus Christ returns.

But the churches will miss it because they are stuck in the mire of religion.

Christmastime Again

It's Christmastime again. I can't believe that I've been saved for so many years now and have been able to be part of so many real Christmases.

It wasn't always so. As a young man who refused to believe in such nonsense such as a god that I couldn't see, feel, or touch, Christmas remained simply a time of tinsel, pretty lights, Thomas Kincaid settings, and presents that you couldn't afford. What a difference a simple prayer can make!

Over the years, I have heard all the reasons of why we shouldn't celebrate Christmas – and I'm sure you've heard your share also. Born in a desire for righteousness but nurtured in a sea of self-righteousness, the razor-sharp arguments contend for an elimination of anything that smacks of red and green. The reasons are prolific. Let's see:

-Jesus wasn't born on December 25th

-It's a pagan holiday
-The Roman Catholics started it.
- No, it was the winter solstice. No, that's not right either. That's on the 21st.
-There's a reference to the Christmas tree as an abomination in the Book of Isaiah
-The only gift giving in the Bible was when Herod cut off John the Baptist's head
- Jesus never said to celebrate His birth; only His

death,

-- etc., etc.

I got it. Really, I do. But aren't there enough commandments in the Bible without having to make up new ones? Does it really make us more righteous to abstain from celebrating Christmas, or does it just make us seem like we're more "enlightened" than the other pagan Christians?

After so many years, there is one thing that I point to that trumps all of those seemingly theological intelligent objections. I have noticed that every year about this time, there is a unique spirit of peace that descends upon the Earth like a softly fallen snow. For this one short period of time each year, people feel something so very different than the rest of the year. Grumpy old men find time to do something nice for others, people in a rush stop long enough to help strangers, strangers reach a sincere hand of friendship to people they've never had the time for before, and children open up in wide-eyed imaginations that are more wonderful than any other time in the year.

It's Christmastime again.

I believe that God in all His loving mercy for mankind reaches down to touch humanity with a taste of the Love of God that we seem to be numb to the rest of the year, just as a reminder that He sent

His only begotten Son as the ultimate Christmas gift to all men everywhere who would accept Him that they may be saved from their sins. It's a taste of what Heaven must be like, sent down from our Heavenly Father who would have all men to be saved. A glimpse at what must be an eternal Christmastime.

> *"For unto us a child is born, unto us a son is given: and the government shall be upon his shoulder: and his name shall be called Wonderful, Counsellor, The mighty God, The everlasting Father, The Prince of Peace."* Isaiah 9:6

In a Stable

I think I know why Jesus was born in a stable and not in a house. This is one of the coolest things I've come across in a long time and I wanted to share it with my friends.

The clue begins with John the Baptist. Zechariah, his father, was of the course of Abia (Luke 1:5), so if you can figure out when the course of Abia ministered in the Temple, you can do the math to figure out when Jesus was born.

The answer is found in 1 Chronicles 24 where David doles out the ministrations of the Temple to the chief rulers of the sons of Aaron. There were 24 of them. Each one was responsible to minister for two different weeks during the year, and all of them had to show up for the three Feasts of the Lord: Passover, Pentecost, and the Feast of Tabernacles, for which all the males of the tribes of Israel were to show up in Jerusalem. The ministrations were given by lot, and Abia (or Abijah) was given the 8th one.

Now considering that the Jewish calendar was a lunar calendar, there were four weeks to a month (28 days), each starting on the New Moon. The first month Abib (or Nissan) started the year sometime in March or April. Since the Lunar Calendar runs differently than our Solar Calendar, dates will shift back and forth.

Abia had the 8th ministration, but you also have to figure in the Feast of Unleavened Bread in the first month and Pentecost in the third, so the course of Abia was on the 10th week, which was during the second week of the third month. The dates would have been from the 8th to the 14th. With me so far?

Zechariah is visited by the angel Gabriel during his ministration in that second week and is told that his wife will conceive. Zechariah finishes his ministration on the 14th day and goes home. Assuming that old Zech' was glad to get home and see his wife, John was probably conceived on or around the 15th day of the third month.

Pregnancy is 40 weeks long, or 10 lunar months. That means that John would have been born during the Feast of Unleavened Bread. It is interesting to note that the Jews to this day traditionally set out a goblet of wine for Elijah as an invited guest during this Feast. John had the spirit of Elijah, so you might say that John showed up right on time.

According to Luke, Jesus was conceived 6 months after John. So if John was conceived during the 3rd month, Jesus had to be conceived during the 9th month, which is right about the time of the Festival of Lights, Hanukah. Since Jesus was the Light of the World, I don't think it would be too much of a stretch to imagine that this was part of the Plan also.

I might also add that the Hebrew word for "feast" actually means "appointed time". God is well able to perfectly engineer His astounding appointments.

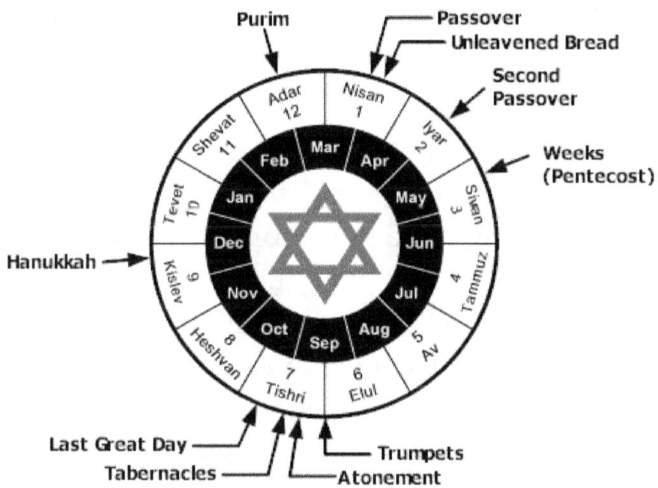

Okay, now it starts getting really cool. If Jesus was conceived in the middle of the 9th month (remember, the cycle all starts when Zechariah went home to his wife on the 15th day), that places His birth at the beginning of the Feast of Tabernacles. The Feast of Tabernacles is a feast of 8 days, the last day being the "great day of the feast", which the Jews call Semini Atzeret. If He was born on the first day of the Feast, then he had to be circumcised on the eighth day, or the great day of the Feast.

No wonder there was no room at the inn! Every Tom, Dick, and Harry (or Ira, David, and Jacob) was crowding out every available place for miles around Jerusalem because they were required to attend the Feast. (Bethlehem is very close to Jerusalem.) I thought everybody was there because of Augustus' taxing, and maybe that is true, but God is not controlled by a heathen emperor but by His own holy appointments.

That makes a lot more sense to me. Bethlehem was a small village and the great bulk of Israelites could not all have been born there, so why was the place so crowded that there was no room at the inn? Because it was the time of the great Festival! What better time to tax them than when they all showed up in one place?

Isaiah said He would be called Immanuel, or "God with us". The word "tabernacle" means dwelling, or in other words, God would "tabernacle" or dwell with us. What better way to fulfill that than to send His Son, Immanuel, as a Savior right at the beginning of this Feast of Tabernacles and confirm it by His circumcision on the great day of that same feast!

Hang on, this gets even cooler!

The Feast of Tabernacles is also called Sukkoth because it commemorated the trek in the Wilderness and the Jews were supposed to spend that time dwelling in temporary booths. Where was Jesus born? In a stable! A temporary dwelling of sorts, not in a house!

Wow. Is that cool?

This may not be some earthshaking revelation that will change your life or anything, but it is one more brick cemented into the wall of our faith that God is not only really there, but He is the Great Architect of the Universe. He is not only able but is active in His dealings with men. He is All-Powerful, omnipotent, and omniscient.

How small is our faith that we do not take Him at His Word for the great and precious promises that He has given us, and to fully believe Him when He says that He not only hears our prayers but will answer them!

> *"Call unto me, and I will answer thee, and show thee great and mighty things, which thou knowest not." (Jeremiah 33:3)*

Corporate Prayer

> *"Blow the trumpet in Zion, sanctify a fast, call a solemn assembly:*
>
> *Gather the people, sanctify the congregation, assemble the elders, gather the children, and those that suck the breasts: let the bridegroom go forth of his chamber, and the bride out of her closet.*
>
> *Let the priests, the ministers of the LORD, weep between the porch and the altar, and let them say, Spare thy people, O LORD, and give not thine heritage to reproach, that the heathen should rule over them: wherefore should they say among the people, Where is their God?*
>
> *Then will the LORD be jealous for his land and pity his people." (Joel 2:15-18)*

Some time ago, I was asked to bring a series of revival messages to a church that was hungry for a fresh outpouring of the Spirit of God. They wanted revival but didn't know how to go about getting one. They had heard about the incredible things that were happening in Africa when I brought these messages over there and hoped that the same thing might happen here.

But wishful thinking and good intentions only work when they are backed up by action. It is not the hearers of the Word…

The secret to revival lies in understanding that

revival is all about winning souls. While that may seem elementary, nevertheless, for that to work, it must be established by serious corporate prayer. Nothing happens without prayer. Jesus said, "Without me, you can do nothing" (John 15:5). But how do we put that into play so that the wheels of revival can start turning?

Most modern Christians (notice I said "modern"?) have their little "quiet time with Jesus". Some have it almost every morning. Others wander through the day tossing up casual requests every now and then. But is this laid-back prayer what God is calling for? Does He not call for a passion like Elijah and determined desperation like the widow with the unjust judge? Have we forgotten how to "storm the Throne of God" as our grandparents did? Does not the Throne of God suffer violence, and the violent take it by force? (Matt. 11:12) Have we allowed our comforts to cast a spirit of slumber upon us, easing us into a lukewarm Gospel that is no Gospel at all?

Regardless of the issues about passionate personal prayer, God calls for the whole church – EVERYBODY – to come together to pray in a serious, solemn assembly of desperate <u>corporate</u> prayer. We're talking about prayer meetings that will lift the roof off the foundations! You want revival? You gotta come get it! Those are the rules. As I have always said, God is a Jew. He makes deals and this is the deal. Take it or leave it.

Months later, there is still no strong drive in this church to come together as a body to cry out to God for revival. The church's prayer meeting consists of a small handful of people relegated to a back room so that it is out of the way of all the other things that are going on at that same time – things that are much more fun and exciting. They sit and politely speak their prayers for a half hour or so, and then go home.

There is no desperation there … yet. It may still come, but the manner in which it will come may not be pretty. Remember, when the Children of Israel got comfortable with their slavery in Egypt, God <u>made</u> them cry out by raising up a Pharaoh who murdered their children. Like it not, agree with it or not, that is what God can and will do to bring us to repentance so that a full Holy Ghost revival can ignite.

God is not fooling around. I have noticed that God will give you a certain space of time to do what He has commanded you. If you don't answer the call, He will move on and find someone else who will.

> *"And they come unto thee as the people cometh, and they sit before thee as my people, and they*

hear thy words, but they will not do them: for with their mouth they show much love, but their heart goes after their covetousness.

And, lo, thou art unto them as a very lovely song of one that hath a pleasant voice and can play well on an instrument: for they hear thy words, but they do them not." (Ezekiel 33:31-32)

Ol' Bill

Well, ol' Bill finally woke up.

Ol' Bill used to come to our little fellowship in the Pizza place in our small town. His son-in-law, Harry, was the pastor there – I say pastor, but it's just a little fellowship where a handful of us gather on Sunday morning to praise the Lord and share the Word. I don't know if most folks would consider it church because there's no steeple or fancy pews with a choir and a pulpit. We just sit around the table and eat Breakfast Pizza while we allow the Lord to speak to us through each other. They don't even label us as a church in the local newspaper - just a Bible study. But that's okay. We got more church going on there on Sunday morning than a whole lot of them bigger cathedrals have all week.

Well, Ol' Bill got himself a parasite overseas back in the '60s, and 17 years later they cut it out of him, all 20 lbs of it ... 'cept they missed some. Well, all these years later, it was back and all plumped up again.

They said they could get it out of him this time, but something went wrong in surgery, and after a day and a half and 100 units of blood, they couldn't get Bill to wake up again. Three weeks later, it wasn't looking too good for Ol' Bill. His nervous system was doing this thing called "storming" where, over and over, his whole body would raise up off the pillow in what looked like a seizure. Looked like he was constipated or something. But Bill wasn't awake. He'd just settle back, eyes half open with a blank stare until the next seizure took him.

The surgeons said he was brain-dead. "Storming" meant that, because of the loss of blood, Bill's brain got fried, and he wasn't coming back. 100% sure, they said. Both of them. Vegetable for life. Time to pull the plug.

Well, we didn't think so. Harry wasn't going to let him go without a fight. It was tough for Bill's wife and daughter to handle. All that high-sounding talk about God, faith, and miracles was starting to seem a little thin. When's the last time there'd been any miracles like that? Anybody ever seen them? How many of your neighbors ever get raised from the dead. Yeah, I know some of 'em look like they came back from the dead, but the real thing?

But Harry knew he had to see this all the way through. It wasn't just for Bill's sake and his family, but the honor of the faith that Harry had preached and claimed was true was at stake. We really needed God to come through on this one.

A bunch of us went up one night and prayed over him. It didn't matter that nothing happened that night. It just mattered that we were taking the battle to the Throne.

Harry and I went up there on a Thursday night by ourselves at 11 pm. Don't ask me why they have visiting hours at 11 pm at night, but we were there and started praying like warriors. Now, I gotta tell you, I never learned how to pray like a Baptist; I was taught that if you really wanted to get something from God, you gotta go get it. So, we commenced to go get it ... at the top of our lungs for an hour. I figured they were going to kick us out because if God didn't raise the dead on that hospital floor, our loud praying was liable to do something real close to it. But nobody said anything – they just let us pray.

I expected Bill to jump up and start dancing around the room at one point, and if he did, I would have been inclined to join him, but nothing happened. I knew, however, that we had broken through something and had touched the Throne of God. We had done everything humanly possible, and our faith wasn't about how much we believed or how many times we repeated a bunch of words, but in the fact that we had busted through to touch the hem of His garment. God was going to heal Bill in His own time so that God got all the glory, not the ones making all the noise in that hospital room, and sure not the doctors who had given up on him.

The deadline was Wednesday to pull the plug, and on Wednesday morning, Bill was still laying there storming away. Millie, Bill's wife, sat there beside his bed asking God for one last time to show her what to do. We had shown up, but where was God?

And then Bill woke up. Just like that. Popped out of the coma, sat up, and said he was hungry. When are they gonna have the surgery?

Yeah, it was a big commotion that happened after that, especially with Millie screaming and all that. It lit the whole place up, all the way from the nurses to the President of the hospital. God showed everyone that He is still there and that He really does hear the prayers of his saints.

But what about the rest of us? America has gone through a spiritual drought for so long that we don't even know how to believe anymore. And when something like this happens, we still question it. We say we believe, but we make sure we have a doctor's appointment in our hand as we raise it up to pray. We call it being prudent; I call it unbelief.

Unbelief doesn't come by choice. It comes from years of letting the raw fires of revival die down to embers so we can get comfortable in church. We've turned God Almighty into a teddy bear and have lost our fear of God so we're no longer scared of Hell, neither are we driven to warn others of it. We have lost our burden to witness to lost souls. Oh, excuse me, it's not "lost souls" anymore, is it? It's "unchurched" nowadays. We don't even have the guts to tell them they're lost.

No more all-night prayer meetings anymore. No more foot-washings. No more fire in our churches. And please, no more hellfire and brimstone messages! We're too comfortable and lazy to do those things like our forefathers did. Besides, we might offend someone if we stood up during our "moment of silence" at football games to pray to God in Heaven. Yeah, "moment of silence" That's one term we got right.

If we have lost our courage to stand up and pray at a football game, how do we think we will be able to stand against the Antichrist? If we are no longer burdened to pray with intensity all night until we get an answer, why do we think God will hear us? If we no longer fear God, how will we be fearless before the enemy? If we no longer witness to others, how do we expect them to get saved, and why would God send lost souls to our church?

We no longer believe in miracles because we have chosen not to.

But you can ask Ol' Bill. He believes.

Oh God

Oh God, where are you? Can you see me? Are you watching? Or are you busy paying attention to 7 billion other people who need you just as much, or much more, than I do?

Have you chosen to set yourself apart from us, just far enough back so that we can almost touch you, but not so close that it would dissolve faith? Sometimes we watch you do miracles, but sometimes all the crying in the world cannot get you to move. Sometimes I can feel the Spirit so strong I feel like dancing; sometimes it feels like the heavens are brass and the door to your presence is slammed shut. Sometimes you feel so close that I feel enveloped in you; sometimes you are so far away that I wonder if you are really there or not.

Belief in God has never been natural for me. The whole concept of God watching over us seemed so foreign to me that it was much easier to believe in the postulates of science than in the hopes of Heaven. Why would God do things this way? How come He doesn't show Himself in the sky so we can all settle this debate once and for all? He does, after all, want everybody to go to Heaven, right? So where exactly is He?

And really, where is Heaven? Is it some far out

place way out in the cosmos or buried in some other dimension? How come it is way out there and we are down here?

We are immersed in the reality of this tangible world and it, therefore, captures our attention. Sometimes it's a lot easier to <u>not</u> believe than to believe, especially when you're praying your guts out and it seems like God is deaf. Heaven can only be hoped for, not seen.

But then there are those times when God reaches down and touches you. Or heals some blind person. Or answers some prayer of yours that was just impossible. Or reaches out and touches you in a place way down in your heart that even you didn't know was there.

Sometimes He just acts like God, and it is unmistakably Him. And then you know.

Pot scrubber for the Lord

I went to bed one evening, tired as usual, and drifted off to sleep almost immediately.

I awoke to find myself opening an invitation that I had just received in the mail. The envelope was made of exquisite vellum paper and inside was a royal invitation made with that same rich paper and printed with pure golden lettering. It was an invitation to the Marriage Supper of the Lamb.

I had never seen such an elegant and rich invitation, and my excitement was palpable. It was the most beautiful thing I had ever seen.

Many of my friends had also received an invitation, and they were all busy sending their white garments to be cleaned and pressed so that they would be absolutely pure without spot or wrinkle. Everyone was excited with anticipation to be attending the greatest event that had ever happened since the beginning of time.

I was so excited that I had to go by the place where the banquet was to be held just to see the place where this wonderful event was going to take place and I noticed a small sign out front: "Help Wanted". "Oh", I thought, "I would love to help in any way I could", so I rushed to the door to offer my services.

Standing to meet me at the door was Jesus. Chattering at a mile a minute, I told him that I would like to apply for the job, how much I would love to help out, and how excited I was at the prospect of being able to be a part of the banquet! I figured that since I had spent so many years in the service of the Lord that surely, He would assign me to something prestigious like the maître d', chief waiter, or something like that. I could picture myself meeting all the guests at the door that would come in and sitting them in their respective seats while I clapped my hands for a waiter to come serve them. This was going to be so cool!

I can still see Jesus quietly standing there, looking at me with those big, black eyes while I chattered away in excitement. He just looked at me and said, "No, we need someone to scrub the pots."

Scrub the pots?

"But Lord, I thought I would qualify for something much better than that. Surely there is a job of some distinction that you would offer me, especially since I have been faithful for so long. Don't you need someone to seat the guests or be in charge of taking the orders?"

"No," He said. "What we need is someone to go down to the dish room and scrub those pots that are crusted over with all that old food and goop.

That's the job that we need to be done."

I looked into the hot, steamy dish room and saw deep stainless-steel sinks piled up to overflowing with all sorts of dirty pots and pans. The old food was caked on some of those pots as much as an inch thick. Others were covered with slimy goop and would have to be scraped and scrubbed and washed for a long time before they would ever come out shiny clean. This was going to be an ugly job.

Well okay, I thought, I'll be the best pot scrubber in the world, and surely the Lord will notice how good I am, and of course, will then elevate me to the much more prestigious job that I deserve.

"No," He said again, reading my innermost thoughts. "You don't get it. That <u>is</u> the job. There are plenty of prima donnas who want to be head waiter and maître d', but we need someone to go down to that hot, sweaty dish room, roll up their sleeves and get filthy dirty, chipping away at those denominational crusts, scrubbing out the old food and stale religious doctrines, and scraping out all the worldly goop that has been smeared all over the pots. It's a nasty job, but somebody has to do it.

"You see", He continued, "if we cook the banquet in dirty pots and pans, maybe no one would notice, but this is the Marriage Supper of the Lamb and those pots have to not only be clean – they have to be sparkling clean. If the pots are not clean, we will not be able to cook the food, and if we cannot serve the dinner, there will be no Marriage Supper of the Lamb."

"Will you go?"

I looked at that pile of pots and pans and realized that this was the job no one else wanted to do. There would be no glory in this job, no accolades of thousands, no recognition of any kind, no pride in my job, position, title, or financial rewards -- but somebody had to do this. It was the job I had volunteered for.

I immediately thought of King David who wrote in Psalm 84 that he would rather be a doorkeeper in the House of the Lord than to dwell in the tents of wickedness. I guess David got the job at the door.

Me? I'm just a pot scrubber for the Lord.

The Passing of Steve Hill

I wonder if the death of Steve Hill ever hit the national press. Should have, but probably didn't.

Steve was the firebrand behind the Brownsville Revival in Pensacola. Millions came through those doors to touch the anointing that had fallen on that church and took whatever residue they could to their churches back home. It lasted around 5 years or so, and then, as all revivals seem to do, the fire faded to coals that hopefully sustained a heat in the churches that, if not as searing, would be longer-lasting. It exploded, it burned, and it faded.

Steve went on to other things around the world, still a firebrand for winning souls, but he contracted cancer and died. Having left the center stage of the Miraculous and Exciting, he had no longer been the darling of the evangelical world, but a slowly fading name amongst his own denomination, and barely recognizable outside it.

And now he is gone.

For me, Steve was a contemporary, so I did not hold him in awe as so many of the younger generation had. He was one of the guys who came from the same roots as I did and preached the same message. We came out of a generation that could see the difference between the Old-Fashioned Gospel that birthed us and the new Love Gospel that the modern church has become so enamored with. But there are fewer of us all the time.

Steve Hill, David Wilkerson, Leonard Ravenhill, and scores of other ministers of fire who preached the Fear of God, did not shrink from painting a picture of Hell in great detail, and demanded holiness and righteousness in our walk with God. There was a difference in their message and a difference in the tenor of their voice – something that is lost on this generation because most have never heard what a message "under the anointing" is like.

Gone. One after the other, they are gone. In their places are polished theological wannabes who faithfully listen to messages on SermonIndex.com so they can copy them and try to mimic the fire and thunder of the past. But the anointing cannot be mimicked or copied – it has to be gotten from down on your knees on the valley floor where your spirit is broken, crucified, and wrung out before Almighty God. It is in complete contrast to the culture of microwave faith and the impatience of this instant, digital generation.

Another revival is coming, but it will not come through a sophisticated modern church but from the cries of a new Gideon Generation. The prophet Joel spoke of an army that would rise just before the Day of the Lord. Rude, crude, outrageous, and on fire, they will rise up with the spirit of Elijah to declare the final coming of the Lord. It will be "Repent or Perish!" all over again.

And Steve – and the others – will be cheering them on.

> *"And the Lord shall utter his voice before his army: for his camp is very great: for he is strong that executeth his word"* (Joel 2:11)

In the Belly of a Whale

> *"And the LORD spake unto the fish, and it vomited out Jonah upon the dry land." (Jonah 2:10)*

Comfort is one of the worst enemies of the Church. It detracts from our original commission by refocusing our attention on ourselves and our blessings and prosperity. Proverbs says that the prosperity of fools shall destroy them (Prov. 1:32). And so, it is with the Church.

Passion is learned through hardship, trials and tribulations, and the sufferings of the Cross. There is no Gethsemane experience without blood; no passion without pain; no victory without a battle. We were not called to the comfort of the Cross but to the sufferings, so that the great deliverance from sin and Hell would be manifest to the world, for as Jesus said, if he would be lifted up, he will draw all men unto him (John 12:32). He was lifted up on that Cross.

The Greek word that Paul uses again and again in this context is "*agonizomai*", which means to struggle, contend, and fight with passion for the victory in the public games where only one contender will win. There is no 2nd place in this contest, no consolation prize, no Purgatory or Limbo to fall back into, no "Ataboy, nice try". We battle in prayer to win. Failure is fatal.

In the parable of the Unjust Judge, the words used to describe the prayer of the widow is translated in the King James as "her continual coming". The actual Greek words mean to push forward until a complete and full end is reached. Our grandfathers in the faith called it "praying it through, all the way through". You prayed, not until you got tired, but until you got an answer.

But in our comfort, our need for that kind of prayer has dissolved. We no longer have the drive and passion that our forefathers had when they fought against all odds to establish the Faith. We don't fight because we don't need to. As a result, our churches are anemic, our pastors compromising, and our religion a "kinder, gentler" version of the old-fashioned Holy Ghost and fire that our fathers knew.

Jonah knew if he prayed like we do, that he would never get out of that whale's belly. He also knew that if he would just contend all the way through to grab hold of the Throne of God, that God would answer. He knew that although he was cast out, if his repentance was deep enough and his prayer strong enough, that he would once again look to God's Temple. (Jonah 2:4) His faith was coupled with the passion of desperation.

It was enough to cause the whale to commit suicide just so Jonah wouldn't get his feet wet.

We have traded our former hunger and desperate prayer for a theological sophistication today that has emasculated the Church. We have programs for everything and books for all sorts of instruction. We know more about human character than ever before, and we have figured out every kind of spiritual program the mind of man can conceive of. We have figured it all out. We have finally arrived.

Leonard Ravenhill once said that the Church has advisors by the carload, but where are the agonizers? Are we so wise and knowledgeable that we no longer have to depend on God?

Our comfort and prosperity have blinded us and led us down a path that leads away from the Cross and straight into the belly of a whale. Perhaps that is what we need so that we can once again look to God's holy Temple.

> *"They that observe lying vanities forsake their own mercy." (Jonah 2:8)*

Confirmation bias:

> *"The tendency of people to favor information that confirms their beliefs or hypotheses. People display this bias when they gather or remember information selectively, or when they interpret it in a biased way. The effect is stronger for emotionally charged issues and for deeply entrenched beliefs.*
>
> *People also tend to interpret ambiguous evidence as supporting their existing position. Biased search, interpretation and memory have been invoked to explain attitude polarization (when a disagreement becomes more extreme even though the different parties are exposed to the same evidence), belief perseverance (when beliefs persist after the evidence for them is shown to be false), the irrational primacy effect (a greater reliance on information encountered early in a series) and illusory correlation (when people falsely perceive an association between two events or situations)."*
>
> *- Wikipedia definition*

In other words, people are going to believe what they want to believe in spite of the facts. While atheists love this kind of gobbledygook to try and explain away the Christian's belief in God, I lean on this more as a signpost directing us to a true and serious belief in Him. I need to know that what I believe in is really real, not something that is projected from my wishful thinking or imagination.

As a young college student, I prided myself on my stone-cold atheism. I felt as if I was much more enlightened than the poor slobs who hung onto the Cross as a crutch. Why they would grasp so desperately for something they could not see, feel, or touch was always beyond my comprehension. Any time that I challenged even the most prodigious of them, including the local pastors, their retorts were anemic and without substance. Leaning on the old, "There must be a God because look at the world around you", was an invalid argument based on a negative, with which you can make a proof of anything.

So why did they hang on to their beliefs so desperately? True, Faith is invisible, but they made it seem nebulous, wispy, and illusory. The only answer I could come up with was that it was a result of social conditioning, an inherent need to believe in something – anything -- to answer the unanswerable questions of Life. As far as I was concerned, it was good for old ladies and little kids but was far beneath the self-respect of a responsible adult.

That is, until God decided to change my mind.

Without getting into a long rendition of the things that have happened to me, suffice it to say that I have been blessed with a lot of supernatural experiences. I don't know why. I guess I just would not have believed otherwise. Who knows? The point is not about the experiences; it is about the fact that He is really, really there.

It is as if you have a room in your house where you can go to meet God. He is sitting right inside there and anytime you go into that room, you can meet with Him. It's as real as real can be. But when your friends come over, they don't believe you. You offer to take them into the room, but they refuse, thinking that you are putting them on a trip. So they never see what you have seen and as a result, they look at you as a nice guy, but a little off balance at best or stupid at worst.

Your friends can quote all the high-sounding science-babble that they want to prove that God does not exist, but you have been in that room, and you have been in His presence, and you KNOW.

The problem lies with the lack of power in the Church today. The Gospel is the "power of God unto Salvation" (Rom. 1:16), so when the Church has no power, it is no better than the world. And what do you have if you have no power?

Our downhill slide began when we wanted to be like the world. Like the Israelites that wanted Saul as a king, we have chosen a worldly rendition of the Gospel which disdained any manifestations of the Spirit that were considered crazy or extreme. I still hear objections about Pentecostals barking like dogs. Excuse me? After 45 years, I have yet to see or hear anything even hinting at stuff like that, nevertheless, there are good seemingly intelligent church people who believe that.

Our irrational fears of being abnormal have neutered us.

Our fear of not being "nice", has stripped us of our holy boldness.

Our preoccupation with "Love", has repelled us from the fear of God.

Our lust for blessings and prosperity has turned us away from a desire for righteousness.

I don't believe because I want to or because I am biased. I believe because I have come face to face with the power of God throughout my 45 years in the Gospel. I refuse to be embarrassed by the working of His power; I refuse to deny the incredible healing miracles I have witnessed, and I make no excuses for the voice of the Lord that has spoken to me on several occasions. Call me crazy, but I believe in the power of God manifested through a Church that rejects the vagaries of the world in favor of a faith that is the very substance of a real living God that you can actually reach out and touch.

If you do not have that, then you need to find a place that does.

No excuses; no apologies; no compromise.

"And my speech and my preaching was not with enticing words of man's wisdom, but in demonstration of the Spirit and of power" (1Corinthians 2:4)

Palm Sunday

Palm Sunday is the traditional day that the Church celebrates Jesus' triumphant entry into Jerusalem the week before He was crucified. I thought I'd share the incredible prophesy that is behind this important event. The prophecy in Daniel 9:24-27 has to be one of the most amazing proofs in the Bible of the absolute inerrancy of the Word of God and the absolute proof that Jesus is really the Christ. If you've not heard this before, you will be amazed.

Jesus Christ was the Passover Lamb and was crucified on the Feast of Passover, the 14th day of the month Nissan. It is interesting that God required the Passover Lamb to be brought in and presented on the 10th day but not killed until the 14th. There can be no other reason than that this was to mirror what Jesus actually did when he was presented to Israel as the Son of David, Messiah, as he entered Jerusalem on the 10th and was later crucified on the 14th. This day of Presentation of the Lamb on Nissan 10 is what Palm Sunday celebrates.

Here's the prophecy:

> *"Know therefore and understand, that from the going forth of the commandment to restore and to build Jerusalem unto the Messiah the Prince shall be seven weeks, and threescore and two weeks: the*

street shall be built again, and the wall, even in troublous times.

(Daniel 9:25)

There are few dates where a king had given a word about Jerusalem, but the only edict that gives any mention of the walls (and gates) of Jerusalem being allowed to be restored was the edict of Artaxerxes in chapter 2 of Nehemiah. This was given in the 20th year of Artaxerxes Longimanus in the month of Nisan of 445 B.C. Using this as a starting date, we should be able to predict the date when the Messiah would be presented to Israel. Since Jesus was the Passover for us, and the Passover lamb was to be presented on Nissan 10th, then the date of His entrance into Jerusalem on Nissan 10th, 32 A.D. should be the date that we are looking to match with Daniel's prophesy.

"Weeks" is translated from the word that means "sevens", or in other words, seven years. The first seven weeks, or 49 years, is what it took to build the Temple. The next 62 weeks plus that 7 equals 69 weeks, or 483 years. Because the Jewish calendar is lunar-based, not solar-based like our Gregorian calendar, it is generally accepted that the prophetic year in Scripture is 360 days (30 days x 12). Using that for our calculation, we come up with 483 x 360 = **173,880 days**. Okay, remember that number!

Now for the next part. From 445 B.C. to 32 A.D. is 476 years (don't count the year 0). 476 X 365 is 173,740 days. Add 116 days for leap years and you get 173,856 days. (Hang on. We're almost there) Finally, we now add the 24 days (both inclusive) from March 14 to April 6, the day of Christ's triumphal entry, and you get a total of **173,880** days!

Amazing. Is there any doubt that God wrote this Bible? Is there any doubt that Jesus Christ is the Lamb slain from the foundation of the world for us? Is there any doubt that not only is He in charge of the affairs of men, but that He will fulfill every promise He has made to us, including His soon-coming return?

One Accord

> *"The Holy Spirit did not come to make them of one accord. He came because they were of one accord ... It is not the music that tunes your piano. It's the piano that makes your music."*
>
> *- A.W. Tozer*

The question, of course, is what would bring all of us into one accord? While the ecclesiastical are always quick to talk about how they believe in unity, they don't do much more than shake hands with their extradenominational brethren. (Extradenominational? Is that a word? It should be. It means to denote those who are outside your own denominational world.)

We might get together once in a blue moon to have a sing-along, but even then, the differences are glaring. Some believe in sedate, cultured music in perfect time while others are boogying to their spirituals; some lean on the Spirit of the old Blood-washed songs while the kids are into Gospel Rock. Then there are the others who look down their theological noses at the rest of us because we are playing with instruments, God forbid!

I would mention the differences in doctrine, but honestly, most folks don't even know what their denomination is supposed to believe. Most of them just make it up along the way and listen to what everyone else tells them. Either that or they have never questioned their church's doctrines enough to establish them on solidly based Scripture. Basically, we all believe in Jesus as the Son of God and that He died for our salvation. How we get that salvation and how we hang on to it are purely divisive issues, but at least we can agree that there is a God up there … somewhere. We're not sure whether there is a Hell or not, but we all agree that there is a Heaven —we're just not agreed on how to get there.

So, what would make us all of one accord? If it is not doctrine or music or styles of worship or even how our faith is supposed to be walked out, then what are we agreed on? And does it really matter?

I believe there is only one thing that can bring the Church into one accord to bring the Holy Spirit down to move for us -- desperation. Raw, searing, bottom-of-our-heart, take-no-prisoners, give-no-excuses plain and simple desperation. That kind of desperation almost always only comes through severe persecution.

Prayer moves God. But if you want God to move, you have to have more drive and passion than speaking or thinking your quiet prayers in a polite manner so that maybe God will hear them and pay attention. If you're desperate, you're not worried about being polite. You only care about one thing –

getting an answer from God! If you want God to move, go move Him! The Throne of God suffers violence! Are you desperate enough to contend in spiritual battle all the way up to the Throne of God and stay there like the widow with the unjust judge until God moves? Are you desperate enough to make sure He not only hears you, but you are willing to drown out everyone else? If you want it to rain, you have to pray like Elijah!

When I preach in Africa, nobody ever talks about what church we are in. All they want is God! Nobody cares what denomination you are stuck in when they are empty and starving for the Holy Spirit of God. When the Church becomes desperate enough to get past our denominational lines and focus on God, that is when we reach the point where we lay down our carnal ways and surrender to a yielded crucified walk in God and let Him lead us to living waters.

We become of one accord only when we are so desperate that it drives us away from Church and to the foot of the Cross.

Legs of Revival

"O worship the Lord in the beauty of holiness: fear before him, all the earth." (Psalms 96:5)

When I look back on the revivals that have happened throughout history, I see certain elements that have always been evident. I've written about many of them, but there are a couple that I don't think I have emphasized enough – holiness and prayer.

It seems like today's messages are all about grace, love, and mercy, instead of holiness in the fear of the Lord. And who could argue against that? What wonderful things they are! How great and wonderful is our Salvation that relies upon the grace, love, and mercy of God. We would be so lost without them!

But is that all there is? Or are we using Grace to minimize the effect of sin, and thereby turning the grace of God into lasciviousness, as it says in Jude 1:4? Have we been so focused on receiving blessings that we have ignored the call to a crucified walk in the sufferings of the Body of Christ? Has this loving modern gospel offered us so much comfort that we have refused the Cross in our pursuit of the Crown?

Every revival in history has been preceded by a time of deep, broken-hearted repentance and remorse for our worldly sinful ways. Desperation, weeping, and howling at the altar as it is described in Joel chapter 2, is what brings God's attention to our cry for revival, not the singing and dancing of superficial worship that bears no marks of the Cross. The Church is complacent in her mediocrity and feels no shame or remorse. She has a "whore's forehead". She refuses to be ashamed (Jeremiah 3:3), and therefore the harvest has been withheld and revival has not come. And without holiness, no man shall see the Lord (Heb. 12:4).

The other thing that is missing is prayer. Revivals are birthed in the labor room of deep, prevailing prayer. The men and women of God that brought forth great moves of God would contend and wrestle in brokenness before God for hours and hours. Four and five hours every day, crying out to God relentlessly was not uncommon. Four or five hours every day! I know of no one in 50 years of ministry that has prayed like that, and yet you will see it in the early labor pains of every revival. How is it that we can be so foolish and cavalier to think that we can just snap our fingers and bring forth a microwave revival – no price, no pain, no tears, no ripping and tearing of our souls. Just waggle our finger in the air with a Howdy Dowdy wooden grin and say "Praise Jesus".

That kind of prayer brought forth men and

women of great power and authority. Know anyone like that today? Me neither. The ones I knew are all dead. All we have left are some nice pastors with nice messages for nice people. There are no John the Baptists left to challenge us, no Elijah's to call down fire, no Martin Luther's, Billy Sundays, Wigglesworth's, or any of those who walked with true God-given authority to call us to our knees in broken repentance and crushing prayer. And yet Jeremiah cried out that the effectiveness of a true prophet of God was seen in his ability to bring the people of God to a place of true repentance (Jeremiah 23:22), not in their ability to entertain us with a message of peace and love.

But what difference will this article make? People will read this and bob their heads up and down like apples in a barrel of water, and then go on the same ways they have been accustomed to. Same ol', same ol'. Like water, we always seek that level that we are comfortable with … until something terrible comes along to rattle us out of our apostasy.

Something terrible is coming that will shake our modern Christianity to the roots with its Pollyanna attitude of personal blessings, sweet Jesus, and a love gospel that excuses sin and dismisses the fear of the Lord. But we don't believe that because we don't want to. And so we will not listen. And as a result, we are destined to face it.

The Lord once told me as I was watching this modern Christianity run in their hypnotic trance straight for the edge of a cliff, that even if they could hear me – which they could not – they will not listen. They are too set in a doctrine that they want to believe and like the children of Israel at the foot of Mt. Sinai, they are given over to the golden calves that they have created for themselves.

> *"And all the people brake off the golden earrings which were in their ears, and brought them unto Aaron.*
>
> *And he received them at their hand, and fashioned it with a graving tool, after he had made it a molten calf: and they said, These be thy gods, O Israel, which brought thee up out of the land of Egypt."*
>
> *(Exodus 32:3-4)*

Biker Rally

I just came back from spending a weekend at a huge Biker Rally in Texas. We were set up there to sell our Cool Bandanas, but there were so many people there (about 100,000) that they needed me to help out with the booth.

Needless to say, it was quite an experience.

As I watched the crowds go by all decked out in their Biker regalia, tattoos, studs, black leather, and biker skullcaps, it felt like I had gone back in time to the old Hippie days. There's a certain fantasy to it all, much like the crowds that get dressed up for Renaissance Festivals, where you enter another world for just a weekend and become something other than your everyday life. I wondered how many put aside their biker garb on Monday and go back to their jobs as secretaries, lawyers, factory workers, and schoolteachers with no one ever knowing the difference.

But just for a weekend, they let loose, became rebels without a cause, and lose themselves in the mystique of being a wild rebel biker.

Now you might think that a Biker Rally with all its reputation for being a wild hedonistic celebration for sin is not the place for a serious Christian – and to a certain extent, you are right. But there I was, stuck for 3 days wondering why in the world did I agree to go down there and get immersed in all this.

And then I remembered Jonah.

True, I hadn't come there to preach as Jonah did – I was there to sell Cool Bandanas -- nevertheless, I was there. And yet it struck me, what sins were these bikers committing that were not to be found in conventional levels of society? Perhaps it's the fact that these people made no bones about their rebelliousness, but rather flaunted it.

Let's face it – sin is sin, regardless of which clothes you put on it. The nominal churchgoers that are comfortable with their lukewarm attendance on Sunday but who never take their Christianity to that deep level of a broken crucified walk in God will wind up in the same Hell as the worst Biker out there.

At least the bikers weren't hypocrites (except maybe on Monday when they put on their wingtips and went back to the office).

I saw the same thing in the '60s. The hippies revolted against the rules set by society and flaunted their rebelliousness just like these bikers today, and yet, when they heard the Truth preached in the power of the Holy Ghost, they came to the altar of repentance by the thousands. But you see, that's the trick – it's got to be the real thing. A dead religion only attracts flies.

I still remember how the established churches rejected the hippies because they didn't fit into their concept of how a Christian should look. I guess God wasn't all that concerned about it because He sent down a great and mighty revival and an incredible outpouring of His Holy Spirit that you won't find in the established churches.

When religions settle into a man-made set of traditional ways, they lose their focus on what is important to God. Pretty soon, they're making the rules instead of God to the exclusion of those who don't fit into their way of thinking. And like modern-day Pharisees, they wonder why people like bikers and hippies reject their version of the Gospel.

On the other hand, if your church is truly on fire and the power of God is pouring out on your services, believe me, souls that are hungry for Truth will come. They don't want some dead tradition – they want the real thing. Only the power of God will attract the lost. If nobody's getting saved at your church every day, maybe the problem is not with them, but with you. Like Jonah, you can miss out on an incredible opportunity to win souls because of stupid traditional ways of thinking.

God had mercy on Jonah; He might not have the same mercy on us.

Fishing

Every good fisherman knows the value of patience.

You can buy the best pole and use the best bait; spend years finding the perfect spot; learn all the techniques that the Pros use; but if the fish ain't biting, they ain't biting! You just have to wait. When they're ready, they'll take the bait.

Being a witness for the Gospel is pretty much the same thing. If someone isn't hungry, you can't cram the Bread of Life down their throat. They'll just spit it up. You can throw their soul in your zeal to get them saved. When they're ready, they'll take the bait, and not before.

Sometimes, when the blinding realization of the Truth of the Gospel hits you, your zeal will make you want to burn up the streets and tell everybody to get saved. You want to just shake them and tell them, "Listen to me! It's real! It's real! It's real! There's a burning Hell beneath your feet and a Kingdom of Heaven above!"

But they don't all want to get saved, do they?

I once asked the Lord why that was. His answer to me was direct and to the point: *"Some people care, and some people don't. It's as simple as that."*

I guess that's pretty much the bottom line. I can't make someone want to get saved and serve the

Lord – only God can do that. My job is to pray.

Just like the fisherman who goes to great lengths to have good equipment and prepare himself, we enable ourselves to win souls by consuming God's Word and diving into prayer so that we will be in the Spirit of the Lord when the time is right. The rest requires patience -- patience and faith that God is in control, knows everybody's situation, and is gauging their hearts.

And so, we pray.

E.M. Bounds once said, "God will not do anything without prayer that He can do with prayer". In other words, we tie the hands of God when we are silent for lost souls, but we open up the way for God to move in supernatural ways when we hammer away at the Throne of God in prayer.

Why then don't we spend more time praying for God to save lost souls? It seems that no matter what church I attend, whenever they get together to pray, all they pray for is themselves. "Mary needs a job; Sally doesn't feel good; I need money; Johnny needs a house; etc. etc." Meanwhile, our altars remain dormant, and people are dropping off into Hell every minute.

Look, I hope everyone feels better, gets that job, or whatever it is that they need, but do you think maybe we're missing something?

Several years ago, when I had just started attending a local church, the Lord spoke to me after one of their "pity prayer sessions" and told me that I had to go tell that Pastor that if they didn't start praying for lost souls, God would not answer their prayers for healing.

My immediate reaction was, "Lord, he's not going to listen to me. He doesn't even know who I am. You gotta make him come to me or I'm not going to tell him anything."

Sure enough, before I could get out the door, here he comes up the aisle to catch me before I left.! There was nowhere to go, so I went ahead and told him. A lot of good it did – they're still consumed with themselves, and their altar is still empty.

Patience, I've learned, is not just hanging around waiting for something to happen. It involves faith that, if you "continue in prayer, and watch therein with thanksgiving", God will hear you, and answer you, and show you great and mighty things that you know not. And when He is ready to move you, you will be ready to be used.

Anything other than that is presumption – and presumption is a sin.

And so here we sit on the riverbank. I got my pole and fresh bait, I've found the best spot, and I'm all set – I'm just waiting for the right time.

Blood, Sweat, and Tears

> *"But avoid foolish questions, and genealogies, and contentions, and strivings about the law: for they are unprofitable and vain." Titus 3:9*

Ah, shucks, Lord. You're takin' all the fun out of it!

We just love to debate, don't we? Swapping doctrinal points of view and arguing about who is right and who is wrong is one of the grand Olympic diversions of Christianity today.

We think everybody's going to Heaven, but we're the only ones that are actually right. How stupid is that?

But it is, in actuality, a sign of apostasy and spiritual pride. If we were really in the place we should be in God, we would be more concerned with lost souls, not theological scholasticism. Ah, but you see, that is the same mistake we have been making since the beginning of time. We like that feeling that we are the ones that are right, and we are willing to argue the point.

What for? Hardly anyone ever becomes convinced, and even if they do, aren't we just making proselytes to strengthen our own feeling of correctness?

Haven't we missed the point?

I like to say that most of the Protestant denominations out there were forged in the fires of revival. Their founders established their churches with blood, sweat, and tears – and that's how it's supposed to be. But there's more to those three words than just a catchy saying.

All moves of God are started with a people that are more interested in God and the winning of lost souls than their own place in God. But you have to be part of something so real that you can feel the power of the Holy Ghost working in you and in your church. It has to be tangible; it has to be electrifying; you have to be able to feel it in the air. You have to know that you know that you know that it's real!

And you have to be so sure that you are willing to shed blood, if need be, for the Gospel that you preach. That takes more than any theological doctrine can provide. There has to be power. You have to be able to touch the Throne of God and feel His Spirit. If you can't, then you will only be venturing a good guess. It's easy to say you believe in something – everybody does that. But it is altogether another thing to be willing to shed your own blood and die to defend it. Those warriors who fought to establish the Gospel had that. We don't.

Sweat comes in the willingness to go out and work the harvest fields to capture lost souls before they end up in a burning Hell. That's not easy, and without an overwhelming love for souls, you'll run out of gas before you get out of the driveway. Most people I have talked to have never prayed anyone through. Man, if you've been going to church all your life and you can count the number of souls that have been saved without taking your shoes off, then brother, you ain't on fire for God. You're just marking time and wasting air.

How few have spent time on their knees laboring all night long in desperate tear-soaked prayer for God to bring a revival, much less fasting their guts out for a move of God? Let me tell you something, God counts tears. And He saves them up in vials that He keeps before His Throne of Mercy.

That's what our forefathers had that brought down the fire of excitement in their churches and established a foundation for the Kingdom of God on this earth. They thanked God for the hard times, the persecutions, and the battles they fought because that's what brings the desperation. And desperation brings revival.

Blood, sweat, and tears. It's not cool, and it sure ain't fun, but it sure beats "Church as Usual".

God Loves Puppies

There is nothing that will soften your heart like a little puppy. If a little puppy can't get you, you can't get got.

It seems that the Lord is very much the same way. He tells us to become like little children or we will not inherit the kingdom of God -- and woe unto you if you offend one His little ones! Little kids and widows have a special place in God's heart.

How unlike us! The things that we esteem highly in our society have more to do with our strengths rather than our weaknesses. Achievements, success, and boldness in business get the gold plaque and the award. Strong personalities prevail in all our human interactions, and those who dominate win the prize, while weaker personalities take a lower place.

This is natural. Life is a competitive place no matter where you are. It is a struggle to survive, and Life isn't always fair. But then, that's the way Life is.

But God is mindful of the weak, the infirm, and those who can't compete.

It doesn't always seem that way, though, does it? Sometimes you wonder why Life is so tough? Is God watching? And if He is, does He realize what you're going through?

And there's always that question in your heart, why me? Does God not like me as much as those who seem to have everything going well? I know that God is completely unbiased, but how come I got the fuzzy end of the lollipop?

Did it ever occur to you that it's not about what you've got, but about what you do with it?

The bright, handsome, talented young man will never have to face the challenges that a retarded, sick, or poor reject has before him. Everything comes easy to him, whereas life seems hard and cruel in comparison to the other. How will that play out when we stand in Judgment? Who overcame the greater challenges in life?

Maybe your weaknesses are your greatest strengths, and your trials are your greatest blessings. In the end, what will matter the most, and which will be the greater testimony?

Don't worry if it seems like you're always looking up at everyone else. Maybe that's a good place to be. Let the titans battle it out for dominance. Look for that secret place of the Most High that is found only in humility and the fear of the Lord like children and widows who desperately need Jesus Christ as their Savior. That's the place where you will find Him.

And yes, God loves puppies.

He Came Seeing

> *"He went his way therefore, and washed, and came seeing."* John 9:7

What a moment! What an incredible moment!

Here this guy had been blind all his life, and Jesus had passed by and, in one moment, had changed his entire life.

Now, why did this guy let someone just come along and plaster spit and mud on his eyes and tell him to go wash in the Pool of Siloam? He could have just been some would-be wanna-be who was promising all kinds of stuff that he couldn't deliver on. Hadn't this guy had a tough enough time sitting on the side of the road all his life begging for scraps to survive without being mocked on top of it? He might have just blown off this Jesus, but he didn't. He had hope.

Hope is something that reaches out past all reason, past all common sense, past everything that the world would condemn us to, and reaches for that slender thread that tells you that there is something more to this life than what you see around you. There has to be something more to life than this temporal existence.

You hope because you can feel it in your soul.

And then there's that incredible moment

when you accept Jesus Christ as your Savior – you wash and all of a sudden, you can see! This man didn't just come back – he came back seeing!

All the colors! All the things that were just sounds before! People's faces! Rocks and trees! Oh, and look at the sky! He didn't just come back – he came back seeing!

The neighbors stood looking in amazement. Was this the same guy? Some said yes, but others said, "I don't know. He looks like him, but he's not the same beggar we used to know. Something has changed about him!"

They didn't get it, did they? Nobody seemed to understand. Even his parents were taken aback. They were so afraid of getting kicked out of the church that they sidestepped the whole question.

But he didn't care. He was saved! He could see! He was alive for the very first time! Really alive! If others didn't understand, it was only because they hadn't tried.

But those who should have known couldn't see what he saw, they couldn't feel what he felt, and since he didn't go to church, then they figured it must not be of God.

Why, herein is a marvelous thing that they couldn't figure it out with their theological expertise, and yet he had been touched by the power of God.

But he didn't have to figure it out – he could see! -- And that's all he needed to know.

If you have never experienced that incredible moment of Salvation, it may look so strange to you. It doesn't follow any set formula that you know about, and you can't feel that Spirit, but if you have hope, if you just have hope, reach out anyway.

And when you do, you will touch the face of God, and you will see as you've never seen before. The Spirit of Life will raise you up from death; it will open your eyes,

... and you will come seeing.

Ah, Christmas!

Ah, it's that season again – Christmas! Children's eyes light up, sparkles and tinsel are seen everywhere, red and green decorate everything, and there's that unmistakable feeling in the air again – it's Christmastime!

It's also time to rehash the same old debate about whether we should celebrate Christmas or not. The argument goes (I'm sure you've heard it by now) that Dec. 25th was set up by Constantine on the winter solstice and is therefore a pagan holiday. (Actually, the solstice is on the 21st, but why let that get in the way of a good argument?)

While that makes for a good debate, I wonder if it misses the entire point? True, Jesus was not born on Dec 25th, so why celebrate it? The Bible indicates that he was born on the first day of the Feast of Tabernacles, but we don't celebrate that, do we? And after all, He told us to celebrate his death, not his birth. And of course, there's the argument about the Christmas tree being pagan idolatry, etc., etc.

All valid points to make an argument for shutting off the season and turning to a more ascetic life. At least we would be technically correct and stripped of anything that smacks of pagan idol worship, amen? (Does that mean we have to tell the kids there's no Santa Claus?)

Sigh. Does it really have to be that way? Is this really such a big deal with God?

My first pastor gave me what I have always thought was the best answer. She acknowledged that although Jesus wasn't born in December, nevertheless, there was a spirit of peace that seemed to blanket the entire world during that season. It was as if God Himself honored Christmas by giving us a taste of His Spirit and suppressing, if only for a short time, much of the ugliness and hate that we had to wade through the rest of the year. It was special, even supernatural. It was Christmas! And just for a season, everything became special, almost magical, and the human psyche with all its arrogance and self-centeredness was pushed into the background. That is, of course, except for the self-righteous Grinches out there.

Perhaps there are bigger issues to be concerned with. It seems to me that the ones who make the biggest noise about this issue are the least likely to show mercy on the lost, but instead are so wrapped up in their own self-righteousness that they have lost sight of the whole purpose of Christmas.

I wonder. Perhaps God allows us to make a mistake on the date so that He can show us in sparkling terms the love that He has for all humanity – the real meaning of Christmas.

"Woe unto you, scribes and Pharisees, hypocrites! for ye have omitted the weightier matters of the law, judgment, mercy, and faith: … Ye blind guides, which strain at a gnat, and swallow a camel." (Matthew 23:23)

Merry Christmas to all

(even the Grinches)

from the Garris family.

Solomon's Wisdom

> *"My mother's children were angry with me; they made me the keeper of the vineyards; but mine own vineyard have I not kept." Song of Solomon*

I guess Ol' Solomon just got too busy. The wisest man in the world, but he forgot where the wisdom came from. The Song of Solomon is his heart-wrenching cry to get back to that place in God that he had lost.

Happens to a lot of us. We get saved, feel the power of God wash us clean, stand up as new creatures in Jesus Christ ... and then we start looking in all sorts of other places for wisdom.

It seems we have developed our own idea of what wisdom is. We read books, listen to lectures (that's a sermon delivered over the pulpit in the flesh), and debate theological points of doctrine in an all-too-human desire to become wise. We figure that the more we know, the wiser we will become.

We convince ourselves that getting a degree in religion will thrust us into a deeper understanding. Four years later, with a degree and a title, we are no closer to wisdom than an Encyclopedia is to genius. Ah, but the piece of paper we got looks good on the wall.

Many would-be scholars, not satisfied with the simplicity of the Gospel, seek after the secret meanings of the Mosaic law in an effort to enhance the New Testament. Having discovered new secret areas of the spiritual, they have now entered into a mystical area of understanding that most of us common people just don't understand. (You wouldn't get it – it's a really deep thing only a chosen few have been enlightened into. Cough, cough.)

The desire to become wise… hmmm. Isn't that the same mistake Eve made?

I don't figure that when I get to the Judgment Bar, some angel is gonna hand me a test with a #2 pencil to fill in the circles to see how much I know. If I get an 85% or better, I go to Heaven; if don't, I go to Hell. (Lord, I sure hope not! Because, like Paul, this poor boy don't know nuthin' but Jesus Christ and Him crucified.)

I don't figure Solomon was much of a theological scholar either – I know David wasn't, and he was the apple of God's eye. For that matter, most of the Apostles were nothing but dumb fishermen. And from what I've read, they weren't even good at that.

So, what's the deal with wisdom? Proverbs says we're supposed to get it with all our getting, so it must be pretty important, but if showing God how smart we are by studying lots of stuff doesn't do it, then what is the secret?

Maybe we should go back and read what an old man said who had tried so hard to be perfect but found himself miserably broken before God: "The fear of the Lord is wisdom" he said, "and to depart from evil is understanding." The secret, in other words, is that instead of puffing yourself up with your knowledge, you have to humble yourself. The complete opposite of what we do.

Solomon finally came to the same conclusion after a whole lot of heartache and misery. He said that, after all was said and done, the whole duty of man was to fear God and keep His commandments.

I guess that's what made him wise.

"Professing themselves to be wise, they became fools…" Romans 1:22

Who Hath Believed Our Report?

> *"Who hath believed our report? And to whom is the arm of the Lord revealed?" Isaiah 53:1*

How is it when we sit and complain of the lackluster performance of the Church that we never seem to find an answer that works? The sinners are not coming, and the saints are leaving. Why is that?

Perhaps we need to initiate a new program that will address their needs. That must be it! The reason they are not coming is that we are not identifying their needs. We are not "relevant" to them. That must be it. Quick, let's search the Internet, comb the Christian bookstore, call up the denominational main office. Let's get a new program to fix this! Don't worry about the cost; it will all be worth it when we see souls flocking to church once more. Oh, I just can't wait.

But wait we shall, for they are still not coming.

I talk to many people outside the church who have a desire for the Lord but refuse to darken the door of any church. Why is that? To be sure, for many it is just the excuse they use to keep from having to give up sin, but for many others, it is because something is missing in the church that they hunger for in the depths of their souls; something beyond smiling faces and friendly attitudes, beyond slick programs designed to address their "needs", beyond the well-meaning intentions of people who appear as cardboard versions with Howdy Dowdy grins. Something real and foundational is missing, but they don't know what it is.

The folks in the church don't get it. They have a hard time understanding why someone who is hungry for God wouldn't come to church. Sure, nobody's perfect and there are always things that could be better, but what better place to iron those things out than in church? The un-churched may not know what is missing, but neither do the churched.

What is missing is the tangible presence of the Holy Spirit and power of God. I am not talking about a perceived presence when we make believe it is here because "where two or more are gathered in His name…." No, I am talking about the radiating glory of God that you can feel. The kind of thing that, when you step inside the sanctuary you know you have entered into the presence of Almighty God and are immersed in that utter knowledge that He is here, right here.

Don't know what I'm talking about? That is no surprise. We have not seen that in a generation or two. But I have to believe that it is coming again.

How will we get there? Not by your slick programs or your theological rationalizations, but by doing what God has been asking you to do all along

– seek His face!

But you've been told. You know. This is not news, it's just not what your flesh wants to hear. The cost of a crucified walk before God means you have to strip away the comforts of the flesh and allow yourself to be broken, to drive yourself into fasting and prayer - the kind of prayer that strives before the altar for hours in deep consuming passion … every day. Oh, you don't pray like that? No, you pray nice little polite prayers … every once in a while. (And you wonder why prayer meetings are so boring?)

And what about reading the Word? Do you not know that the Word of God is where you get your power from to pray? The Word of God is the source of all power, faith, and passion. It is the fountainhead of your walk in God. It is where it all starts. Oh, you don't read that much? I see. Surprise, surprise.

Is it a small wonder that the church is anemic? We are supposed to be the salt of the earth, but we have lost our savor. But have you not heard? Were you not told? Oh yes you heard, but you did not hearken. You know, but you don't get it. You can recite it by rote, but when it comes to that point where you actually have to do something, you fall back on your never-ending excuses.

All revivals and every move of God must be birthed in prayer and fasting that is fueled by reading the Word of God. That requires you to pay a price.

The question is not whether or not it has been revealed to you and you have believed the report. The question is whether or not you want it that bad.

> *"They on the rock are they, which, when they hear, receive the word with joy; and these have no root, which for a while believe, and in time of temptation fall away."* (Luke 8:13)

Forming Light

> *"I form the light, and create darkness: I make peace, and create evil: I the LORD do all these things." (Isaiah 45:7)*

Here is something interesting. The Word of God says that He formed light, not created it. Somehow, I always figured that everything was dark, and then God flipped on the switch and created light. Not so. He is light. It was already there. There is no darkness in Him. Wow, does that have tremendous implications!

I had to know more, so I looked up the word, "*yatsar*". It means to form or fashion, to devise, to frame. The word implies initiation as well as structuring. It is used to designate a potter as he squeezes and molds clay into a vessel. I know that one has just struck you! The Potter fashioned us in the same way that He has fashioned and formed Light! In Isaiah 29:16, the Bible says,

> *"Surely your turning of things upside down shall be esteemed as the potter's clay: for shall the work say of him that made it, He made me not? or shall the thing framed say of him that framed it, He had no understanding?"*

The "potter's" in "the potter's clay" is the same word, as in the word "framed." It is the same in many other scriptures and suggests that the prophets of God brought a "formed" or "shaped" message to Israel.

The great implication is that the things of Light were not created from scratch, but always existed. He just fashioned it into what we see.

Going further, I looked up "create darkness." Sure enough, the word "bara" means to create from scratch. Bara emphasizes the initiation of the object, not manipulating it from its original creation. Darkness did not always exist. Darkness was created.

If you are like me, all of a sudden, your mind just stretches out to all sorts of theological implications, not the least of which are the ramifications to Particle Physics. It changes the whole view of the Beginning and what was before it … and what created it.

Light is Life and Darkness is Death. Just as Death did not exist until sin entered the world, so it, along with Hell, will be cast into the Lake of Fire and will forever cease to exist anymore. Satan may have rule over this carnal world, and he may seem to have a dominant presence here, but just as it was not always so, so shall it end. His lie to humanity is that he is in charge and dominates the affairs of Man, but God will have the last word.

It was, after all, His Word that started it all.

In a Field of Barley

"And after him was Eleazar the son of Dodo, the Ahohite, who was one of the three mighties. He was with David at Pasdammim, and there the Philistines were gathered together to battle, where was a parcel of ground full of barley; and the people fled from before the Philistines.

And they set themselves in the midst of that parcel, and delivered it, and slew the Philistines; and the LORD saved them by a great deliverance." (1Ch 11:12-14)

There comes a time in your Christian life when you have had enough of good intentions, fair speeches, and repetitive platitudes. There comes a time when you are ready to plant your feet on solid ground and are ready to fight. No more talk; it is time to DO something.

I do not believe that David and his two companions honestly thought they were going to live through this battle. This was way past what David faced with Goliath. After all, the enemy was so fearsome that the entire army of Israel ran in terror. It says in 2nd Samuel 23 that they only came back after it was safe.

But while the situation had changed, the principles had not. They gripped their swords and drew a line in the ground beyond which they would not move. Three guys standing against incredibly overwhelming odds … no let me take that back. No bookie in Las Vegas would even give you that much of a spread – there were NO odds. Not a chance. Adios, amigo!

But there comes a time when you have had enough talk. Come Hell or high water; win, lose, or draw, there comes a time when you are ready to stand and fight for the honor of God. No, I don't believe they thought they would win – they just didn't care. This was not their battle; it was the Lord's. It was not up to the circumstances, the odds, or the facts – it was up to God Almighty. It didn't matter what the outcome would be; what mattered was that they stood.

I have some friends like that, who yell out into the face of the enemy, "To Hell with the devil! Damn the torpedoes! I will not back down, I will not back up, I will not compromise, and I will not run!" God often puts his servants in situations like that to give them the opportunity to trust Him no matter what. Like Jonathon scrambling up the rocks to take on the enemy, they hang onto the promise that *"there is no restraint to the LORD to save by many or by few."*

Champions are forged in times of utter desperation and sharpened by absolute reliance upon the salvation of God. There are times when the only thing that is sure is the Rock upon which you stand. Those are the times of victory.

True Holy Ghost revivals are birthed out of the same womb. There has to be a time when the Church has had enough of "church as usual", enough of that sing-song Pollyanna Gospel our churches are so full of. Enough of the worn-out platitudes of peace, love, blessings, and how much Jesus loves us. When will the Church fall under the conviction of the Holy Spirit to repent of their Laodicean ways, their preponderance of worldly flash and glitter, and seek to the old paths, look to the old ways of old-fashioned, broken repentance at the altar for God to forgive us for having "church" instead of what He called us to?

When we reach that point, we will then have the courage to stand in that field of barley.

A Shadow in the Noon Day

> *"Take counsel, execute judgment; make thy shadow as the night in the midst of the noonday; hide the outcasts; betray not him that wandereth." (Isaiah 16:3)*

There comes a time when you are called to make a stand against things that are wrong and answer the call to fight against the oppression of the weak and innocent. God calls you to first take counsel and understand what you are doing and why. Whenever you stand up to resist the oppression of darkness, you need to understand that you will pay a price for your convictions. But stand anyway because it is the right thing to do. You may not win, you may not come out of it unhurt, you may pay a higher price than you'd like to, but there is a point when, knowing and realizing what the price may be, you make that decision anyway. It is a determined call that rises out of your soul that cries out that this is right and that is wrong, and you refuse to give in to the intimidation of iniquity. Count the cost and make a decision that you will stand for that which is right.

When you do stand, it will be in stark contrast to the landscape around you – as the shadow of night in the midst of the bright noon day. There is no mistaking who you are, what you are doing, and what you are standing for. There is a boldness to righteousness that fuels a faith that is defiant. It is a David kind of faith -- the kind he took out into the field to defy Goliath; the kind that galvanized his feet with his two friends and defy the entire Philistine army. It is the type of defiant faith that Jonathan declared as he rose to scramble up the rocks that *"there is no restraint to the LORD to save by many or by few."* These were men of faith to whom the odds did not matter. It was not about winning or losing, or personal safety or advantage. It was not about blessings and prosperity. It was that "Damn the torpedoes!" call to a battle for righteousness. What were the odds against David when he and his two friends faced down an army that was so fearsome that the entire army of Israel had fled? Who cares? They stood to fight for the honor of God, and it didn't matter what the odds were! Did it matter to Jonathan that there were only two swords among all the Israelites to fight over 100,000 men of war? Not hardly. To men such as these, the victory belongs only to God. The only thing that matters is what is right.

God thrusts us into opportunities of challenge to strengthen and forge us into men and women of conviction, champions of righteousness, and defenders of the Faith. It is not an opportunity to be missed. Our weapon is the Word of God, our armor is our faith and our righteousness, and our determination is fueled by the zeal of the Lord of Hosts. We stand, not because we count the odds, but because it is right.

We have been called to hold up the Blood-Stained Banner in the battle for the greatest cause of all time. Let us stand in such contrast to the world that we are as a great shadow of night in the midst of a glaring noonday sun that we may give refuge to a lost and dying world that has been beaten down with the forces of darkness, where victory has been stolen and trampled upon, where hope is but a faint glimmer in a dark world, and where courage is in great demand.

About the Author

Dalen Garris has been in ministry since 1970 during the Jesus Movement in California. In 1997, he began a radio broadcast that ultimately spread to dozens of countries, from Israel and Saudi Arabia to Africa and the Philippines. His program, *Fire in the Hole,* was selected for broadcast four times a week for several years across North America on the Sky Angel network as the Voice of Jerusalem.

A newspaper column followed, for which he has written over 700 articles, which have been published in local newspapers and Christian magazines in several countries. He has also written over a dozen books and several booklets.

Since 2004, he has been lighting the fires of revival in churches spread across sub-Saharan Africa. During the course of 17 years, he has preached in over 1,000 churches and has seen hundreds of them set on fire and explode with growth, and hundreds of new ones planted across Africa.

Hundreds of people have been supernaturally healed during the healing lines that so often sprang up during these revival meetings, and tens of thousands have been saved. And the fires are still burning.

Because of his work across Africa, Dalen Garris was awarded an honorary Doctorate in 2017 by the Northwestern Christian University of Florida.

Dr. Garris currently lives with Cindy, his wife of 43 years, in Waxahachie and is still heavily involved with churches across Africa.

His pressing hope is in seeing this powerful move of God in Africa ignite us here in America to see those same revival services that made such an explosion in Africa. He believes that this upcoming generation will be the Gideon Generation that will usher in this last, great revival that he has preached about for so many years.

Brother Dale, as he is known across Africa, has settled in Waxahachie, Texas, with his wife and three grown daughters and their children. You can contact him and find his pamphlets, books, videos, and podcasts at www.RevivalFire.org.

If you would like him to speak at your church or organization, please contact us for times and schedules. We do not charge, nor will we ever charge, to preach the Gospel anywhere in the world.

He is willing to take this message anywhere people are hungry for a God-given, Holy Ghost revival.

Books by Dalen Garris:

Available at: www.Revivalfre.org/books

Four Steps to Revival

Do You Have Eternal Security?

Standing in the Gap

Two Covenants

Fire in the Hole

Revival Campaigns

The Kenya Diaries

A Trumpet in Nigeria

A Scent of Rain

Into the Heart of Darkness

Fire and Rain

Revival Campaigns in Africa – 2019

The Battle for Nigeria

A Match in Dry Grass

A Light in the Bush

A Voice in the Wilderness series:

vol. 1, the Journey Begins

vol. 2, the Early Years

vol. 3, Prophet Rising

vol. 4, Revival in the Wings

vol. 5, Sound of an Abundance of Rain

vol. 6, Watchman, What of the Night?

vol. 7, Mud and Heroes

vol. 8, Ashes in the Morning

vol. 9, Shaking the Olive Tree

Booklets by Dalen Garris

- *Available at: www.Revivalfire.org/booklets/*

A Volcano in Cape Verde

Tanzania, 2011

Nigeria, 2012

Planting a Seed in Liberia

A Whisper in the Wind

Finishing What We Started

Calvinism Critiqued

RevivalFire Ministries
PO Box 822
Waxahachie, TX 75168
dale@revivalfire.org

RevivalFire.org

www.ingramcontent.com/pod-product-compliance
Lightning Source LLC
LaVergne TN
LVHW010621100826
845148LV00014B/3058
* 9 7 8 1 7 3 7 7 9 4 4 1 7 *